Second Edition

First Semester
Success

Learning Strategies and Motivation for
Your First Semester (or Any Semester) of College

Second Edition

First Semester

Success

Learning Strategies and Motivation for
Your First Semester (or Any Semester) of College

Arden B. Hamer, Ed.D.

WORD ASSOCIATION PUBLISHERS
www.wordassociation.com
1.800.827.7903

ISBN: 978-1-63385-272-3

Library of Congress Control Number: 2013916505

Designed and published by
Word Association Publishers
205 Fifth Avenue
Tarentum, Pennsylvania 15084

www.wordassociation.com
1.800.827.7903

In memory of my parents, John and Helen Beswarick, and with gratitude to Dale, Lisa, and Megan for their boundless love and encouragement.

Table of Contents

Section One: Before the Semester Begins 13

1. High School vs. College 15

2. Advice from Students Who Know the Ropes 16

3. Things to Consider as You Prepare for the Semester 17

4. Get Connected Early 18

5. Financial Literacy 19

6. Roadblocks and Detours 20

7. Secretaries will Be Your Best Friends 21

8. Motivation and Goal-setting 22

9. Friends 23

10. Four Ingredients for Learning 24

11. Three Keys to a Successful Semester 25

Section Two: First Third of the Semester 27

12. Study Cycle 29

13. First Week of the Semester 30

14. The Importance of the Syllabus 31

15. Go to Class! 32

16. Get Involved, But Not Too Involved 33

17. Concrete, Hands-on Learning Strategies 34

18. Homework and Assignments vs. Studying 35

19. What Should I DO When I Study? 36

20. Time Management Tools: A Review 38

21. Students' Favorite Strategy: Review Lecture Notes after Class .. 39

22. Academic Reading Process: Step I 40

23. Academic Reading Process: Step II 42

24. Academic Reading Process: Step III 43

25. Q & A as a Reading Strategy 44

26. Annotation or Margin Notes 45

27. What about E-books 46

28. Recitation: A Strategy for All Occasions 47

29. Be Purposeful, Persistent, Prepared 48

30. Dealing with Sickness and Other Problems 49

31. Effective Lecture Notes: In the Classroom 50

32. Effective Lecture Notes: Outside the Classroom 51

33. Effective Lecture Notes: Expand and Complete the Learning
    Process 52

34. The Next Step: Study Guides 53

35. Lecture Notes: Different Delivery Systems 54

36. Hard-to-understand Professors 56

Section Three: Middle Third of the Semester **57**

37. To-Do Lists = Done! 59

38. Setting False Deadlines 60

39. Collaboration between Writer and Reader 61

40. Signal Words 62

41. Characteristics of a Successful Student 63

42. Student Scenario 64

43. Studying for Midterm Exams 65

44. Preparing for a Major Exam 67

45. Motivational Goal Setting 69

46. We Are What We Repeatedly Do… 70

47. You Are Capable, But Are You Willing? 71

48. Studying: Active vs. Passive 72

49. Evaluating and Reacting to Midterm Grades 73

50. Persevere for the Second Half 75

51. The Big Picture 76

52. Look for Associations and Connections 77

53. Overcoming Procrastination 78

54. Dealing with Distractions 79

55. Overcoming the Mid-Semester Slump 80

56. Not Just Your Grandma's Kitchen Timer 81

57. Common Mix-Ups 82

58. Plan Your Work and Work Your Plan 83

59. More Effective Academic Reading—Two Quick Steps 84

60. Distributed Practice 85

61. How to Handle Low (or Lack of) Interest in a Subject 86

Section Four: Final Third of the Semester **87**

62. R–R–R–R–R–R 89

63. What Are Your HABITS? 90

64. Learning through Your Senses: Visual 91

65. Learning through Your Senses: Auditory 92

66. Learning through Your Senses: Muscle Movement 93

67. Learning through Your Senses: Multisensory 94

68. Mnemonics 95

69. Final Weeks of the Semester 96

70. One Point Can Make a Difference 97

71. Knowing vs. Understanding 98

72. Learning is Cumulative—Success is Habitual 99

73. Student Scenario 100

74. Strategic Reading 101

75. Study = Learning + Review 102

76. Time Management for the End of the Semester 103

77. There is No Such Thing as Multi-tasking 104

78. Don't Take Too Much of a BREAK Over Thanksgiving Break . 105

79. After Thanksgiving Break 106

80. The Purpose of Exams—Not Just Torture 107

81. Successful Essay Exam Answers 108

82. Strategies for Multiple Choice Exams 109

83. Preparing for Final Exams 110

84. What to Do If You Are Not Prepared for Finals! 111

85. 'Twas the Week before Finals and All through the Dorms... 112

86. Survival Guide: Finals Week 113

Section Five: After the Semester has Ended **115**

87. What to Do at the End of the Semester 117

88. Grades Are Posted—Now What? 118

89. What to Do if You Do Not Agree with a Semester Grade 119

Section Six: Looking Forward **121**

90. Roadblocks to Success and Strategies for Change 123

91. Preparing for the Start of a New Semester 126

92. How to Raise Your Grade Point Average 127

93. Take a Break Over Spring Break 128

94. Don't Succumb to Spring Fever 129

95. Summer Days: Keep Learning 130

96. Transfer Credits from Other Schools 131

97. Word about Technology 132

98. Tips for Online Classes 133

99. Surviving Condensed Classes 134

100. Motivational Quotes 135

Introduction

To the Freshman:

This book is written for you as you embark on your academic career. Going to college is exciting and, at the same time, rather scary. You are entering a new world of education—one in which you are the main person responsible for your success. This book follows you on your journey through the first semester with brief entries tailored to the specific events and challenges that will likely occur throughout the year.

- Section One starts with some things to consider before you even go to your first class.

- Section Two introduces you to college-level learning and gives you information about how to read and learn from your textbooks and from classroom lectures. Interspersed with information on concrete learning is information about time management and motivation.

- Section Three deals with what happens during the middle portion of the semester and includes information on dealing with the "mid-semester slump," midterm exams, and grades, along with reviews of learning and motivation strategies.

- Section Four covers the final third of the semester, with information about finals and test-taking strategies, and more on motivation.

- Section Five is brief and discusses what to do after the semester has ended, including evaluating your grades and your learning and then planning for the next semester.

- Section Six deals with miscellaneous items such as how to handle spring break, how to raise your grade point average, and how to deal with common roadblocks to academic success.

This second edition has been updated to address the influence of technology in education and learning. Specific websites and programs are not identified because what is available now can change rapidly. The basic principles about how we learn, however, will not.

My hope is that you will read an entry every week day and use the information as soon as possible in your studies. Don't let this restrict you, however—you should also feel free to read ahead so that you know what to expect and to reread earlier pages to reinforce what you already learned.

Each semester is different with different classes and a different schedule. When you start the next semester, start the book again. One of the keys to learning and motivation is repetition—we must keep reminding ourselves what we need to do to be successful!

Good luck and enjoy the experience!

To the "Not-Quite-so-Successful" Returning Student:

If you are not happy with your performance so far in your academic career, this book is also for you. It will give you information that you need to improve all aspects of your learning, including time management and motivation. The concrete information about learning will change how you approach learning and will make your studying more effective. You will read that one key element of academic success (or any success) is habit. Get into the habit of using successful study and learning strategies. Whenever a new strategy is introduced in this book, try it that day and then keep at it. Spend some time thinking about your motivation—why are you in college and what do you hope to gain? Analyze what you did in the past that created a roadblock to your success and resolve to make changes. Set a goal for the semester—either a specific grade point average or a specific grade for each course. This book will give you the information you need to make positive changes and to reach your goal.

Good luck! Stay positive and keep your goal in sight.

Section One
Before the Semester Begins

Things to think about:

High school vs. college

Advice from upperclassmen

Motivation

Learning

Keys to a successful semester

High school *vs.* College   **1**

There are two major differences between college and high school (and many smaller ones!) that students, especially freshmen, need to keep in mind.

The first major difference is exactly who is responsible for your learning. In high school your teachers taught in class and planned activities to help you learn. In college, the professors are experts in their fields and are sharing their knowledge with you. While they often plan class activities that help students learn, for the most part, the learning is your responsibility and happens outside of class. Throughout this book you will learn exactly what you can do to make this learning happen, even when you are simply in your room or the library.

The second major difference is time management. In high school every day was basically the same, and your time was organized for you. Now each day may have a different schedule, and there is no one around telling you when to get up, when to study, when to eat, and when to go to bed. Not to mention when to get your laundry done! There are several tools you can use to keep everything straight and get everything done:

At the start of each new semester, get a monthly calendar and write down major exam dates and due dates for papers and projects.

Also, at the beginning of each semester, sketch out your weekly schedule, including classes and any regular weekly appointment such as meetings or work. You can then see the week and decide when you have time to study, eat, exercise, and do that laundry.

Use a weekly planner to keep track of your appointments and other things you need to do each week.

Make a daily to-do list to prioritize and detail what you need to accomplish each day.

These tools will help you manage your time so that you have time for both fun and studying. Be sure to start using them at the beginning of the semester and get in the habit of doing so. You will find that you feel much more organized and less stressed, and you are not missing assignments or rushing at the last minute to finish things.

In my teaching I often work with upper-class students who are, unfortunately, on probation because their grades are not high enough. At the end of each semester, I ask them to write a paper about what they have learned about achieving academic success. Year after year there are several themes that students report as helpful:

Sleep: More and more studies are showing the importance of sleep in many activities, one of which is learning. It is difficult to concentrate and learn when you are tired.

Chunking: Instead of working with a huge amount of material at once, break it down into small "chunks" and learn those parts, then put the information together into the whole picture. (Of course, each chunk must be a logical section of material.)

Review notes as soon as possible after each class: Students who did this were amazed at how well they learned the material and how well they then did on exams.

Academics are more important than socializing: Most of the students who were on probation reported that in the previous semester they had spent more time socializing than studying. Once their priorities were switched and they put more importance on their academics, their grades greatly improved.

Go to class: Almost every student on probation did not do this. You just cannot miss class. The problem is that one absence leads to another. After an absence you do not feel as comfortable or a part of the class, making it easier to skip class again. So even if the professor does not take attendance, go to class

In addition to deciding which clothes to pack and what meal plan to purchase, there are many other things to consider as you start a new semester:

How will you manage your time and keep track of assignments? You will have many professors giving you assignments and exam dates, and you will need more than your memory to keep them all straight. As mentioned earlier, some things that are helpful are: (1) a monthly calendar where you can write all major papers, projects and exams; with this you can see the semester and plan your time better; (2) a weekly date book where you can write all smaller assignments as well as your plans or goals for that day or week; and (3) a weekly schedule of all classes and regular meetings, work, exercise times, etc., so that you can effectively plan when you will study.

What are your goals for the semester? If you are a returning student, think about your previous grades and set a goal slightly higher. If you are a freshman, examine your classes and be realistic. You want your goal to challenge you, but also to be achievable.

What are you going to do to achieve your semester grade goal? Think about how you learn. Plan early to use active, concrete learning strategies.

What road blocks might get in the way of your academic success? How will you deal with them? Have a concrete plan in place before temptation crops up.

Enjoy the semester and be sure that plans are in place for your success!

4

It is important to connect electronically with your school as soon as you have committed to attend.

E-mail
You will be given an e-mail address sometime during the summer. Get into the habit of checking your college e-mail, particularly toward the beginning of the semester. Important information will be disseminated this way. Also, many professors send class e-mails with course information and sometimes an early assignment.

Institution Website
Look for a special section for new students. This could include move-in instructions, general policy information (student conduct, alcohol policy, etc.) that you are expected to read to prepare for the semester.

Textbooks
You can probably learn which textbooks you need for your courses through the college book store website. You may be able to pre-buy them, but do not write in them or remove any cellophane wrapping until *after* the first class in case the professor has changed his or her mind or in case you change your schedule.

Many students buy textbooks from outside websites. Make sure you get the correct edition.

Computer Support/Operating System
Find out what computer support is available and what operating system the school uses. In many cases you can get programs for free or at a reduced student rate.

See what online storage is available for papers and projects. Many professors will expect you to turn in papers electronically and will expect that they are stored in the cloud, not on a flash drive or hard drive that can crash.

One topic rarely addressed is financial literacy. College is generally a time when you will not have a lot of money. If you want or need to work, consider getting a job on campus. There are several advantages: you will be close to your job, your employers will be willing to work around your class schedule and will understand when you have exams, and sometimes it is possible to get in some study time during work hours. If you do a good job, it is likely you can keep the job through your college career, possibly even in the summer. There should be a student employment office on campus to help with your search.

Here are some other things to consider:

Do NOT sign up for a credit card as a fund raiser for campus organizations. Even if you do not ever use the card, it will appear on your credit history. You are starting to build your own credit rating now, and promotional credit cards will hurt your record.

Think about buying used textbooks, renting books, or sharing books. Textbooks are a necessity but a huge expense.

If you have loans or financial aid, be sure that you understand the terms, conditions, and payment plan. It is important to know how many years or semesters the loan covers and if summers count as a semester. Also, is there a certain grade point average you must maintain or a certain number of credits you must successfully complete each academic year?

Do it right the first time. Avoid failing or withdrawing from classes if possible so that you do not have to take (and pay for!) the class a second time.

Be thoughtful and careful in your selection of a major. After the first year or so, changing your major could add a semester or more onto the semesters you need to graduate. Most colleges offer career exploration classes and have a career center that will work with you to select a major.

You do NOT need a $5 cup of "designer" coffee or smoothie every day. Save that for a treat on Friday or after a major exam. Regular coffee or juice (or even water) is just as good and a lot cheaper.

6

Roadblocks
and Detours

College is an entirely new experience, so it is hard to anticipate what roadblocks and obstacles you might encounter. While you plan for smooth sailing, it is a good idea to anticipate what you might do if an obstacle is in your path. Everyone is different, but there are some common obstacles that students face:

- Sleeping in, missing class, or choosing to do something else other than going to class

- Missing an exam or not starting to study early enough

- Getting sick

- Problems at home that distract from studies

- Problems with boyfriends or girlfriends

- Choosing to socialize instead of study

- Lack of interest in a subject

These issues will be addressed multiple times throughout the book but start the semester with the resolve to avoid these problems as much as possible instead of having to recover from them.

It goes without saying that you should treat everyone with respect and the way you would like to be treated. (This is a good life lesson no matter what you are doing in life!) At institutions of higher education, as in every big business, the inner workings are very complex, and it takes many people working together to get things done.

One thing you need to know is that the academic department and administrative secretaries are the people who know how things work—they are the ones who can go into the computer system to make changes or fix things. While your professors are in charge of their classes, the secretaries are the ones who understand the system and who can often help you out in a jam. They can answer your questions or call someone else if they do not know the answer.

Likewise, the custodians and maintenance people can be lifesavers. In the end you never know who will be able to help you when you have a problem. So—treat everyone kindly, not just because of what they may be able to do for you but because everyone deserves to be treated well.

8 | Motivation and Goal-Setting

One way you can keep yourself on track and motivated throughout the semester is by setting goals. These can be short-term (for the day or week), mid-length (month, semester), or long-term (year, several years, etc.).

Whatever the length, a good, workable goal has several characteristics:

1 There is a time limit.

2 It is measurable.

3 It is attainable.

Here are some examples of goals with these three characteristics:

- This week I will go to all my classes.

- Today I will select a topic for my research paper.

- By the end of the month I will have my paper completed.

- This month I will complete the process to change my major.

- At the end of this semester I will be on the Dean's List.

If you are having trouble with motivation and procrastination, setting goals is a great tool to help. The goal will help keep you focused. Of course, you need to frequently look at the goal and remind yourself what you are trying to do! By successfully completing a goal, you are motivated to keep working and accomplish something else. So, after meeting your goal, immediately set a new goal.

If you do not achieve your goal, you should revise it, reset it, and start again. Success never happens if you quit! So . . . what is your goal for the first week of classes?

Take a minute to write a goal for the semester either here or on a note card. Then, review it often!

Friends

9

You will make many new friends in college—some may become your friends for life. One quick piece of advice: you don't have to find your lifelong best friend during the first week of classes. Take your time. Look for people who have similar interests, values, and goals as you. Most importantly, look for friends who will care about your success and make you a better person. Don't become friends with someone who will tempt you to skip class, not study, and get into trouble. A true friend will want the best for you and will help you achieve your goals.

Here are two questions to think about:

1. What qualities do you want to have in a friend?

2. What qualities do you possess that make you a good friend?

23

Four Ingredients
for Learning

Often students are surprised that they get a low grade on an exam even after they have "gone over their notes" several times and read the textbook. BUT—learning requires **varied** and **repeated** exposure over **time** and **self-testing**. Let's look at those four ingredients:

Varied: You have to do different strategies in order to truly learn. For example, read the textbook, read your lecture notes, quiz yourself on what you read, put the information into a study guide, add color, make a practice test, have someone quiz you, and give the answers out loud. That's eight different forms of study right there, and they're certainly not all your options.

Repeated: In order to really know something, you have to study it many times, not just once. It takes a lot of repetition to get the information firmly in your memory. And this repetition must be done over time (the next ingredient).

Over time: Knowledge takes time to be set permanently in your memory—the night before the exam just won't work! So as you are going over and over the material, spread it out over a week or weeks. Reviewing difficult material 20 minutes a day, every day, during the semester works wonders. You will be amazed at how much you know! (Of course, this is above and beyond your regular studying.)

Self-testing: It is necessary to practice recalling the information from your memory, just as you will be asked to do on the exam. See if you can restate what you have read or reviewed without looking back at your notes or book.

These four things put together will lead you to successful learning and a better grade on the next exam. It might seem like a lot, but you can do it and the result is worth it.

There are three simple things that you can do to be sure that you have a successful semester:

1. Go to class.
This is common sense, but it is easy to start to skip classes and then it becomes a habit. If you find yourself skipping, evaluate how you are spending time . Another way to look at it is that you have paid for the class. You would never go to the gas station, give the attendant $40, and then not put the gas in your car. It is the same when you skip class—you paid for the information, so why not get it!

2. Review your notes after each class.
After class review your notes as soon as possible, definitely before the next class. A future entry will list various strategies you can use with your notes, but for now be sure to read over them several times per week. At least once a week go over all of your notes on material that will be on the next exam.

3. Use recitation
Recitation means to restate something in your own words from memory. Once you have reviewed your notes, close your notebook and explain what you learned in your own words. You might explain it to yourself out loud if you're alone, explain it to a friend or roommate, or write it down as though you were speaking it. Don't try to do this with five pages of notes all at once; rather, divide the notes into manageable, logical segments.

Some of this already seems repetitious but remember our definition of learning (see entry #10). You need to constantly remind yourself what to do until it becomes second nature (or a habit!).

Section Two

First Third of the Semester

Things to think about:

What to do the first week

How to manage your time

How to study and learn

How to read and learn from your textbooks

Taking and learning from lecture notes

During the first week of classes it might seem that you do not have a lot of work. This will change quickly, so it is important to get into productive study habits now.

You can think of each week as a cycle that you are going to work through, and then at the beginning of the next week start it over again. For a class that meets 3 times a week, the study cycle is:

Go to class > review your notes > read the textbook > Go to class > review your notes > read the textbook > Go to class > review your notes > read the textbook > REPEAT from beginning

If you have a class that meets twice a week, you should still review your notes at least three times a week. If you have a class that meets just once a week, you will need to review your notes three or four times between classes.

In future pages you will learn information about what to actually do while you are reviewing your notes—it needs to be more than just rereading!

For now, get into the habit of reviewing your lecture notes as soon as possible after class and reading your textbook before and/or after class to check and review information.

13 First week of the Semester

Don't be fooled by the laid-back atmosphere of the first week of the semester. Even though many professors start lecturing immediately, there doesn't seem to be a lot to do. Everyone is getting settled, getting used to their semester schedule, catching up with friends they have not seen since last semester, or making new friends. This relaxed atmosphere will change rapidly, so be prepared.

There are several things you should be doing:

- Be sure you have all the books and supplies that you need.

- Take some time to look through your books: How is each book organized? What study aids are included? What will make the book easy or difficult to learn from?

- Get your calendar and write in all your major assignments, exams, and papers.

- Look at your class schedule and plan when you will study, and then start to follow the plan,

- Set a goal for the semester (for example, a grade point average that you would like to attain), write the goal on a notecard, and post it where you will see it every day.

- Begin to study now—review notes after each class, read ahead in your textbooks, and create study guides.

Before you know it, it will be the middle of the semester. If you have started strong and stayed strong, things should be going well and you will be pleased with your grades and class performance. Remember: it is easier to keep up than to catch up!

The Importance
of the Syllabus

During the first week of the semester you should receive a syllabus for each of your classes or be directed to where you can find one online. This is an important document and should be kept with your class papers. Each institution has different policies, but in general you should find the following information in the syllabus:

Who the professor is and how to contact him or her; some will respond to e-mail, while others want to see you personally in his or her office

Location of the professor's office and office hours

Attendance policy

How you will be evaluated

Schedule of exams throughout semester

How the final grade will be calculated—which exams or assignments are worth more weight than others and how the grades are divided (for example, 90%–100% for an A, or 93%–100%)

Whether the professor accepts late assignments

What happens if you miss an exam

What the textbooks are and whether they are optional or required

Daily readings and assignments (use the syllabus each class to be sure you are keeping up)

Finally, keep the syllabus after the class has ended. If you should ever decide to transfer, the syllabus will be important in helping your new school evaluate your courses and decide which credits will transfer.

Go to Class!

It cannot be said enough: GO TO CLASS! This is the basis for your academic success. If the professor does not require attendance, there is great temptation to just not go. But one skipped class leads to another—it is a slippery slope!

What happens is, when you miss a class, you do not feel as comfortable the next time you attend. You will not necessarily know what is going on or what they talked about in the missed class. This, then, tempts you to miss another class.

One strategy that helps my students with attendance is to make a weekly chart listing all classes for that week. Then cross off each class you attend. The act of crossing them off, and the visual of seeing the week complete will help you remember to go to class and keep you motivated. Then do the same thing for the next week.

It really comes down to being in the <u>habit</u> of going to class. You will find that you feel more comfortable in the class when you regularly attend, and your grades will reflect your dedication.

There is more to your college experience than classes. It is important to get connected to the campus and your fellow students. Take your time to see what groups are available—what groups have interests similar to yours. There probably will be an organization or club fair sometime toward the beginning of the semester where groups have informational tables to let new students know about that organization.

But don't join everything and get overwhelmed. Budget your time and energy. For this first semester, your main priority is your studies. Possibly limit yourself to one or two organizations. And do not volunteer to be in charge of the big social event right away!

One important connection you should make is in your major. There is probably a club or group dedicated to that major that will have meetings and events where you can get to meet other students in the same major. Upper-class students will be an invaluable source of information about classes, professors, extracurricular opportunities, internships, etc.

Activities are an important part of your college experience, just choose wisely!

The more actively involved you are with the material you want to learn, the more efficiently you will learn it. Learning will take a lot longer if you sit and passively read or review your lecture notes. Instead, try some hands-on activities. By adding movement, color, or noise, you will increase your retention and shorten your learning time. Here are some ideas:

- When reading your textbook, make notes in the margin or take separate notes.

- Read some passages out loud.

- With textbook material or lecture notes, transfer the material you want to learn into a study guide.

- Make study cards.

- Add color to any of the above.

- Practice remembering—close your book or notebook and restate what you just read.

- Teach someone else.

- Make a practice test and trade with a friend.

- Take your notebook to the gym with you and review on the treadmill or exercise bike.

- Record a summary of the material and listen while you are driving or walking.

- Sing your notes to a beat.

- Create your own Power Point slides to explain the information.

The idea is to add some variety to your studying. Use multiple strategies to learn the material. And don't forget to space your studying out over time!

Homework and Assignments
vs. Studying

Many college students don't understand the difference between **homework** and **assignments** and **studying.** Generally, in college there are very few **assignments** where your work is graded. So it might seem that you do not have that much work to do. What no one mentions is that you are expected to be **studying** all the time, and that **studying** is your "**homework.**"

So what should you do when studying? Here are some ideas:

Review your notes as soon as possible after each class.

Once a week review all the notes that will be on the next exam.

Read the textbook for the class. Maybe take some notes from the book or add information to your lecture notes.

If available, do practice problems and take practice tests.

Use recitation—after reviewing your notes, close your notebook and see what you can remember. Then check and correct your information.

Make study guides such as concept maps, study cards, and review charts.

It is important to do a variety of strategies and to **study** each subject several times during the week.

The work is hard but the reward is great!

What Should
I DO When I Study?

This is a question many students have! You know you need to "study" and you may even have heard the rule of thumb about studying 2 hours for every hour in class. When I am working with students on probation they say they are going to study "more" or "harder" but they often don't know what to actually DO.

Remember that to learn something, you need to be exposed to it in a variety of ways, at several different study sessions, and spread over some extended time period.

Here are some more in-depth ideas for different concrete things to DO when you are studying:

Of course, you are going to read over your lecture notes. While doing that, be sure you understand everything and that all the information is clear. If there is something you are not sure of, check back in the textbook. This should be done as soon after class as possible—before the next lecture.

If needed, write down questions and then ask for clarification before the next class or during your professor's office hours.

Break down the information in your notes into logical sections or chunks. Read that section, then close your notebook and restate the information in your own words. Check yourself and do it again if you are not 100% correct.

Take important terms, people, and events from your notes and put them on study cards with the term on front and definition and additional information on the back. You can add more information from your textbook. Then quiz yourself. Remember to restate the information before checking the back of the card.

Create study guides from the information.

Form a study group and either teach the information to the others or take turns quizzing each other.

Take advantage of any online study guides or practice tests.

Make your own practice test and take it a few days later or switch with a friend.

Remember, you need to do several of these strategies, and they need to be spread out over the time period leading up to the exam. They will not work during an all-nighter before the exam!

Pick one strategy and get started!

Time Management Tools:
A Review

The semester is now in full swing. Take a minute to think about how you are managing your time and your assignments. Here is a review of the four time-management tools described earlier:

#1—Semester calendar

At the beginning of each semester, write all your exams, major papers and projects and important social events on a monthly calendar. Post this and check it often to see the big picture of the semester. Look for when you have clusters of exams and major things due, and then plan your life around those.

#2—General weekly schedule

Graph out your class schedule for the semester. Add in anything that happens regularly on a weekly basis such as work or meetings. This will give you an idea of when you can study and how to fit in other activities. This weekly schedule needs to become a habit.

#3—Daily planner

Write down daily assignments as they are given by your professors or listed in the syllabus. This is where you will plan each individual week including special events, appointments, etc.

#4—To-do list

Use this to plan your goals for each day. Write this out either before bed or first thing in the morning. This will help each day be more purposeful and productive. If you have a busy week, you can make a to-do list for each day of the week either Sunday night or Monday morning. This helps reduce stress because you plan exactly what you will do and when you will do it.

Many students feel that they don't want to be so scheduled and want to be able to "go with the flow." By planning your time, you will actually have more free time and be able to enjoy it more because you are not always thinking about what you should be doing. Try it!

In the learning strategies course I teach, one strategy that is mentioned over and over is to review lecture notes as soon as possible after class, at least before the next class meeting. In my students' final papers, students report that doing so makes a major improvement in their learning and retention of the information. Here are some things to do when you review your notes:

Make sure they are clear and understandable. Add information if needed.

If they are particularly messy or unclear, rewrite them.

Make any corrections needed.

Add important or clarifying information from the textbook.

After reading them, use chunking and recitation—choose one topic, cover the information, see how much you can remember, and then check yourself. Then move on to the next topic.

If there is some information that is particularly difficult, create a study guide.

THEN—at least once a week review all the notes that will be on the next test.

It is also helpful to do a quick review of the previous lecture notes before the next class begins.

If you do these things, you will notice a major difference in your learning and then in your grades.

One major difference in college is the amount and the difficulty of the reading you are asked to do for your classes. Think of academic reading as a process with several stages, not as an isolated event. The following three entries give you some strategies to make your academic reading more effective.

There are several things you can do **before** you start to read that will greatly enhance your comprehension and retention. Here are some ideas:

Preview the assignment, chapter, book, journal article. Look at the learning objectives, major heading and subheadings, bold-print words, pictures, charts, graphs, etc. By doing this you will see the entire scope of the information. Then, as you read, you will be able to see how all the information fits together.

Think about what you already know about this subject. The more you know about something, the easier it is to learn new material. So, prepare your memory to latch on to the new information.

If you don't know anything about what you are reading, previewing will help you start to **build background knowledge.** You can also take a few minutes and look on the Internet for some basic information.

Plan to remember what you are reading. I know this sounds simple, but how many times do you sit down to read and your main thought is just to get it over with? Have a positive attitude!

Make a reading plan. Don't try to squeeze a long chapter into a short period of time. Decide how many sections of the material you will be able to read and comprehend in the allotted time and read that. If you finish and have a few minutes left, review what you read instead of forging ahead.

Eliminate distractions. Turn off the TV, e-mail, IM, social media, your cell phone—all those things that will break your concentration. You can reconnect with everyone in an hour.

Take some breaks. Don't try to read for several straight hours. You do need to give your brain a break and get refreshed. Just remember—the break is a few minutes, not several hours or days!

There are quite a number of things you can do **while** you are reading to increase concentration, comprehension, and retention.

You probably already do several of them:

- Monitor your comprehension.
- Reread if necessary.
- Perhaps read something out loud.

Here are some other things you can try:

- Practice recitation (restate in your own words from memory).
- Write annotations or margin notes (look a few pages ahead for details about this).
- Visualize what you are reading (if the subject works for this).
- Associate what you are reading with what you already know.
- Think about how what you are reading fits into the overall picture of the chapter or subject.

If you find you do not understand, you can try the following:

- Review the overall organization of the chapter or book.
- Reread the previous paragraphs.
- Review the meaning of important words.
- Skim the material first to get the "gist," and then reread in more detail.

Even though you have finished reading an assignment, there is one more quick thing you <u>should</u> do and several strategies you <u>can</u> do **after** you are done reading to improve your learning.

<u>You should:</u>

Review—Take a few minutes to look back and think about what you have read. Reread your margin notes or your separate notes. Look at the bold print headings. Try to summarize the chapter objectives. Taking just a few minutes to do this will help the information stay in your memory.

If you need more intense learning, **<u>you can</u>:**

Make a study guide from the information

Write out the answers or information that goes with the learning objectives at the beginning of the chapter.

Form a study group, assign each person a section, and then teach it to each other.

Take any online or textbook quizzes or practice tests available.

25

Forming questions and then reading to find the answer is a very effective reading strategy. Many psychology textbooks have started to include questions at the beginning of each section to guide your reading. Learning objectives in the form of questions at the beginning of chapters do the same thing.

You can also ask questions on your own. It is especially effective in textbooks that do not have a lot of guidance for the reader. Here is what to do:

- Take the bold print heading and turn it into a question. You can do so by following the news reporter's guide—add "Who, What, Why, When, or Where" to the heading.

- Read to find the answer.

To expand on this, you can write the question and then write your answer rather than just thinking about it.

The interesting thing is that even if the section does not answer your question, your reading focus and comprehension are still improved because you were looking for the answer. If this happens, go back and rephrase your question after reading, and then answer it.

Here are some examples from a history chapter about The Enlightenment:

Heading: The Popularization of Science
Question: How did science become popular? What happened?

Heading: The Legacy of Locke and Newton
Question: Who were Locke and Newton? What did they do? Why were they famous?

Heading: The Impact of Travel Literature
Question: What is travel literature? What was its impact?

Happy reading and learning!

Annotation
or Margin Notes

Another way you can increase your reading efficiency and retention is by writing brief notes in the margins of your textbooks. These are called annotations or margin notes. They are short—maybe just a few key words—and summarize the important information contained in a paragraph or section.

By using this strategy while you read, you are becoming a much more active reader. This will result in higher comprehension and retention.

Here is what to do:

Read the paragraph or section. **1**

Think about what the important information is that you need to remember. **2**

Condense that information into a few key words. **3**

Write the words in the margin of the page near where you found the information. **4**

There are other ways you can mark your pages:

Write numbers beside where items are listed.

Write "def" beside where an important word is defined.

Draw a small concept map or chart in a white space to help you understand something.

Keep in mind that this is a new way to read and may be uncomfortable at first. But isn't any change uncomfortable? Give it time and you will wonder how you ever read without a pen or pencil in your hand!

By using this strategy you are ensuring that you will be actively involved with the information, and you are doing much more than simply letting the words run through your mind.

What About E-Books?

Textbooks are a crucial tool for learning. Most professors expect that you will have read and understood information in the book before class. They then build on that material in the lecture and class. The price of textbooks is skyrocketing, and many professors work to control the cost to the student through e-books and online articles. This presents several advantages and disadvantages:

Advantages:

You, the student, save money.

You don't have to carry around heavy books – all you need is your portable device.

Publishers are refining e-books to aid in learning. You can make margin notes, highlight, take self-quizzes, define terms, and find other learning tools to help you read and understand the content.

Disadvantages:

If the book is from a publisher, at semester's end the book will disappear from your device. You cannot keep it for future reference. You cannot share with other students or sell it back at the end of the semester.

You may have to work harder to be actively involved with the information. Be prepared to take separate notes.

You may have a more difficult time previewing the chapter and getting an overview of the organization. This can be done, however, and greatly improves comprehension.

Distractions are a major problem. It is too easy to flip to e-mail or social media. Turn these off while you are studying!

Of course, there is always the chance your device will malfunction. Know you school's computer lab hours and the office for technology support.

NOTE: Textbooks and online documents are evolving rapidly. One trend is to use books and documents that are available for free online, bypassing the major publishers. Given the wide variety of materials you may be assigned, it will be even more important to have multiple reading and learning strategies available.

There is one study strategy that is extremely helpful in just about all learning situations: RECITATION.

Recitation means to restate in your own words from memory.

This is so powerful because you are practicing recalling the information just as you would on an exam or when you need the knowledge on the job. It is much better that just rereading your textbook assignments or passively reviewing your lecture notes.

Here is how you can use recitation:

When reading, pause and recite what you have just read without looking. If you can do this, move forward. If not, go back and reread and then try again.

When reviewing lecture notes, read a section, close your notebook and see if you can recite what you just reviewed. As above, move forward if you can, review again if you cannot.

When using study cards, read the front of the card, think about the information on the back, and then check yourself. If you are correct, set the card aside. If you are incorrect, put the card in a separate pile and go through those until you get them all correct. Tomorrow, go through them again.

In math, practice doing problems without referring to your notes or book, then check your answers and procedures.

When learning a second language, be sure to practice recalling and speaking the new words, don't just "look over them."

If you have made a review chart, cover the information and see what you can remember.

Some of my students in the past have misspelled this word and written "resuscitation" which means to revive from apparent death. In a sense this is correct – using recitation can revive your studying and give your learning new life!

Now practice recitation. Cover this page and see what you can remember about what you have read. Then check your recall. Good luck!

You can enhance your academic success through these three **P**'s

1 Be **P**urposeful: Daily, make choices that will help you with your studies. For example, go to the library after class to review your notes instead of going back to bed for a nap. Stay after class to ask a question instead of meeting up with your friend. Do some extra studying even though the exam is two weeks away. In general, live each day so that what you do is helping you reach your goal of academic success. (This doesn't mean there is no time for fun! If you are managing your time well, you can do both.)

2 Be **P**ersistent: Don't give up. Even when you are feeling discouraged and your studying does not seem to be going smoothly, keep going. Bounce back after an exam grade that might be lower than you had hoped. Analyze your day-to-day studying and exam preparation and make changes. Work at staying healthy, motivated, and current in all your classes for the entire semester.

3 Be **P**repared: Don't wait until the last minute to finish a paper. The printer will always run out of ink at that time. Leave yourself some leeway for emergencies. But being prepared also is important in case an opportunity comes your way. You want to be ready when the great job opens or when you are asked to participate in an academic event that will add to your résumé. People who have great "luck" are always prepared when that "luck" happens.

Getting sick during the semester is definitely a problem. Even if it is "just" a cold, you do not feel like going to class or studying. One obvious answer is to always be current with your work, if not working ahead. For example, if you are reviewing and studying your lecture notes after each class, you will be ready for an exam and one or two days off will not be a problem.

If you have been to every class, participated, and your professor knows that you are a dedicated student, he or she will be more willing to work with you than if you have presented yourself as an uninterested student.

I prefer for my students to contact me by e-mail when they are sick or having some other difficulty so that I know why they are not there. Of course there are limits. You can only have so many flat tires in one semester!

Germs run rampant throughout the dorms, so in order to stay healthy be sure to:

- Wash your hands
- Eat properly
- Get enough sleep
- Exercise

If you do get sick, contact your professor, take care of yourself so that you get better quickly, and get the class notes from a student who you suspect will earn an A in the course.

(A quick note about getting someone else's notes—recopy the notes in your own style into your notebook and add information from the textbook to be sure you understand. Studying from someone else's notes is not effective!)

31

Effective Lecture Notes:
In the Classroom

When you are taking lecture notes, you are actually creating a new document that you will use to study and learn the class material. Here are some suggestions you can use in the classroom to improve your lecture notes:

Take a good seat. The best location is in the middle T—the front few rows and straight down the room in front of the professor. You will have better eye contact and better hearing. Don't be afraid to move from distractions like windows, radiators, and chatting students.

Quickly review the previous notes while waiting for class to begin. Each lecture builds on the previous knowledge.

Date your notes so you can easily find a section when reviewing. Number the pages if using a loose-leaf notebook.

Leave a lot of blank space. This will give your eye some space to rest, and the organization will be clearer. It will also leave you some room in case you need to add more information.

Abbreviations are good because they help you write faster but be sure you will remember them a month or more later. You could leave some space and complete the word later as you review.

Only write on the right side of the notebook. Then if you need to add more information you have the blank left page.

Look for the professor's organization of the material. Watch for verbal and nonverbal signals to know what is important, how many points there are, etc.

Write down everything the professor writes on the board.

If the professor uses PowerPoint and you have access to the slides before class, print them out and take your notes directly on that paper.

Remember, you are creating an entirely new text that you will need to use for learning. Be sure your notes are as "workable" as possible!

The quality of your lecture notes starts outside the class with one important thing—read the textbook before class. This gives you a preview of the topic, the organization and the words the professor will be using.

Then, the main part of your learning happens after the class has ended. In a traditional lecture class, you are gathering information during class, but the actual learning happens individually after class. So . . . what should you do? How can you learn all the information you wrote down during class?

Here are some basic ideas to use during your initial review of your notes:

Read over your notes as soon as possible after class ■

Make any corrections ■

Be sure they are clear—if you cannot understand something now, the chance of understanding later is slim ■

Identify your questions ■

Check in the textbook for any information you can add to your notes ■

Begin to learn the information: ■

    Chunk into logical topics ☐

    Use recitation—read each section, then look away and repeat in your own words what you just read ☐

At least once a week, review all the notes that will be on the next exam, again using chunking and recitation. ■

So far we have examined strategies for taking effective notes in and out of class. The last entry discussed reviewing your notes daily in logical chunks and using recitation. These strategies are sufficient for the immediate review, but you are far from done.

First of all, you must review all of the notes that are going to be on the next exam at least once a week, if not more. You need constant repetition and review in order to completely master them. Also, you need to use some different strategies with your notes, above and beyond reviewing them and using recitation.

Here are some ideas:

Do something with your notes that requires you to physically manipulate the information and reorganize it. These could include making concept maps (mind maps), review charts, time lines, or some other format.

Add color.

Make study cards and take them with you for spur-of-the-moment study.

Form a study group and compare notes, then teach each other the material or quiz each other.

Make a practice test, put it aside for a week or so, and then take it yourself.

Make use of any study aids in the textbook or online—practice quizzes, terms to know, review questions, etc.

Make use of any professor review sessions, supplemental instruction, or walk-in tutoring offered by your institution.

Finally—review, review, review, and use recitation all the time. You MUST be able to explain the information in your own words with complete recall for the exam!

Good luck! (But with good preparation you won't need luck.)

Other than going to class, reading the textbook, and reviewing your lecture notes, what else can you do to increase your learning?

One strategy is to create study guides. There are a variety of formats:

Outlines

Study cards

Question and Answer

Concept maps or mind maps

Review charts

Time lines

Venn diagrams (compare and contrast)

Study guides are versatile. They can be made from any or all the following:

Textbook chapters

Lecture notes

A combination of the textbook and lecture notes

Small sections of material you are having difficulty with

All the material to be covered on an exam

Any material you need to organize and understand more clearly

Making the study guide is one major learning session. Then studying and reviewing from the guide using recitation is another. If you are making a study guide for an exam, start early and then have several days to review. Other guides, such as outlines, study cards, and Q&A, can be made as you are learning throughout the weeks.

Keep in mind that you are not limited to just one. You can do as much as you need to do to be successful in your learning. The sky is the limit!

Format: Traditional spoken lecture

Challenges: It is easy to drift off, look at your phone, or think about something else when attending a traditional lecture.

Strategies:

- Bring a drink or hard candy with you to keep you alert.
- Read the textbook and review previous notes so that you are familiar with the information.
- Sit up front.
- Every time your mind wanders, make a hash mark on the top of your page when you bring your attention back to the lecture. Over time you will become more aware of your mind wandering and be more attentive.
- Be sure to continue to write—that will keep you involved.

Format: PowerPoint

Challenges: Without realizing it, sometimes professors move too quickly through the slides because they do not have to write anything.

Strategies:

- Politely ask the professor to slow down. (Everyone else in the class is thinking the same thing!)
- If possible, print out the slides ahead of time and take notes directly on the slides. Use the format where the slides are down the left side of the page and there is room for notes on the right.
- Review the strategies for the traditional lecture.

Format: Flipped Classroom

Description: Students are expected to listen or watch recorded lectures before class. Students then come to class prepared to discuss and work with the lecture content.

Challenges: The responsibility to listen to the lecture is entirely the student's, and it is easy not to do it. If the recorded lecture is only audio with no visual cues, it's going to be more difficult to follow and understand content.

Strategies:

Take notes and study like you would in a traditional lecture.

Don't wait until the last minute in case there is something you do not understand.

Go back and re-listen or re-watch the lecture after class to clarify important or complex information.

Format: Smart Classroom

Description: Everyone in the room can connect to the computer and projector.

Challenges: Be sure you are knowledgeable about how the system works.

Strategies:

Download documents and shared group work.

Be prepared to contribute. Expect the professor to have in-class questions and activities with students' responses shown on the screen.

Take notes as in a traditional lecture.

Whatever you decide to do, go to class! Listen! Write!

Hard-to-understand Professors

It is quite probable that you will have a professor with a heavy accent whose first language is not English. There are several things you can do to help you understand the lecture:

- Read the textbook before class so that you are familiar with the words. (I hope you expected that this would be the first suggestion!)

- Talk with the professor before, after, or outside of class so that you can start to get accustomed to his or her accent. Go to office hours with some sort of question about the class, just as an excuse to talk.

- Go through the textbook after class to fill in your notes.

- Meet with fellow students after class to combine lecture notes.

- Talk with a student who previously had the professor for some tips.

- If available, go to tutoring for the class, so you can hear someone else explain the material.

Just don't give up—after a week or so you will be accustomed to his or her speech and it will be easier to understand.

Section Three
Middle Third of the Semester

Things to think about:

Persevering

Evaluating and honing your learning and studying

Midterm exams

Midterm grades

Procrastination

As a college student you have a lot of things to do for many different classes. This can be overwhelming! One way to stay on top of things is to make a to-do list each morning for that day. (Some people find it helpful to write it at night before they go to bed.) This strategy will help you organize your day and make sure that you complete what needs to be done. You can also prioritize your list so that you do the most important things first. It is a great motivator to cross things off as they are completed and then crumple the list and throw it away at the end of the day!

If it is a very busy time and you are feeling overwhelmed, a weekly to-do list is also helpful. Take a sheet of paper and make columns—one for each day of the week. Then think about what you have scheduled (classes, practices, etc.) and decide what is the best day and time to complete each task. Write each task under the day you plan to do it. Now you can quit worrying about getting things done because you know exactly when you will do them.

There are always more things to do than there is time, so to-do lists will help you use your time well, help you not to forget something, and eliminate some of the stress of getting it all done.

One very simple way to keep up-to-date with your assignments and avoid last-minute panic and procrastination is to set false deadlines. When you have an assignment due, set your deadline a day or more before the real deadline.

Tragedy is always ready to strike. Here are some sample problems that may come up:

- No computer paper
- No money on debit or ID card for printing
- No ink for printer
- Getting sick the night before paper due
- Roommate getting sick night before paper due

You get the point—many problems can arise.

Having your work done ahead of time relieves stress and gives you time to be sure the work is done to the best of your ability. Try it!

As you are reading your textbooks and other material, you are not alone. The writer is working along with you. A good writer keeps you, the reader, in mind and leaves clues so that his or her point is easy to follow. There are several types of clues:

Signal words: These are small words that help you follow along with the writer's ideas. Some examples are *first, second, next, finally, on the other hand, but,* and *however.* The next entry explains this more in depth.

Bold print: The writer uses bold print to let you know that something is important.

Margin notes: Many textbooks explain important information in the margins.

White space: It is easier to read something that has some breaks so that your eyes get a rest. White space can also be used to set apart information that is important or indicate a break in the information or change of direction.

Your job, as the reader, is to be on the alert for these clues. As you are reading, be seeking meaning and looking for how the writer has organized and presented the information.

Interestingly, this idea will improve your own writing. If you keep your reader in mind and write so that the reader can follow along, your writing will be more clear and understandable.

40   Signal Words

One way the writer helps the reader follow along is through the use of signal words. These are small words not related to the topic that alert the reader to the following:

- Are there several points? How many?
- Is the writer changing topics?
- Is the writer giving an opposing point of view?
- Is the information presented in chronological order?
- Does one part of the information cause the other, or vice versa?
- Is the author comparing and/or contrasting information?

Here are some examples of signal words:

- Multiple points: *numbers, first, second, next, then, last, finally*
- Opposing points of view: *but, on the other hand, conversely*
- Chronological order: *in order, first, second, then, finally*
- Cause and effect: *because of, caused by, resulting in*
- Compare/contrast: *likewise, similarly, the opposite, in contrast, on the other hand*

Of course there are many other words—these are just a few examples to give you the idea. Just keep in mind that the writer is choosing words carefully to help you, the reader, understand his or her ideas. Your job as the reader is to be aware of signal words and watch for them as you read.

In my classes we often talk about the characteristics of a successful student. The most common suggestions from my students include:

Motivated
Determined
Persistent
Optimistic
Organized
Focused
Puts forth effort
Works hard

You probably have displayed many of these characteristics in other settings such as sports or other activities you enjoy. Reflect on what you did to be successful at the sport or activity (for example, you practiced, didn't give up, analyzed your mistakes and adjusted, etc.) and then think about how you can transfer these attitudes and strategies to an academic setting.

Another strategy is to focus on your goals—why are you in college? You can set a goal for the semester (for example: be on the Dean's List, choose a major or career) and then post that goal where you can see it every day to remind yourself of what you want to achieve.

Take a second and write down your answers to the following:

1.) What positive characteristics do you already possess?

2.) How are you exhibiting these characteristics in your everyday actions?

3.) What positive characteristics would you like to develop that would help you be successful?

4.) What is ONE thing you can start to do TODAY to make a positive change or continue to succeed?

One of my students e-mailed me asking to be excused from my class because he had to study for exams in two other classes. He wrote that he had stayed up all night studying and was not quite ready for the exams. This student was on a sports team, but could not participate until he was in academic good-standing.

My response to this student was that he did not understand learning, time management, or how his body works.

First, he could not learn the information he needed to know the night before the exam. Learning takes time. He should have been learning the information over the past five weeks of the semester, not just the night before.

Second, he was not using his time properly. Again, he should have been studying all along. He is getting into a very bad habit by skipping one class to study for another.

Third, he needs sleep. Sleep is important to memory—both for the learning and the output of information. Also, because he was tired he was not able to think properly during both exams, and it took him more than a day to get back on track.

How did things turn out? One exam has not yet been returned. My student earned an A on the second exam, but made the statement that he hoped the final was not cumulative because he already had forgotten everything he had studied.

So the moral of this story is:

Understand how you learn.

Manage your time.

Get proper sleep.

Hope you have an understanding professor who will help you have sustained academic success by giving you the information explained above.

We are nearing the midpoint of the semester, and exam dates are starting to pile up. What is the best way to study for an exam?

Start with the ideas that you have been learning all along. When you reviewed your notes after each class (you have been doing this, right?) you started the learning process. Then, when you reviewed all of the notes for the class once or twice a week you kept that information fresh in your memory. Now it is time to look at the big picture and review for the exam. Here are some ideas:

Start one week before the exam. List all the topics to be covered. Then do more than one or all the following:

Make a study schedule for the week: ■

On day one, study the first topic. ☐

On day two, study the second topic and review the first. ☐

On day three, study the third topic and review the first and second. ☐

Repeat until all topics have been studied and reviewed several times. Continue to review until the day of the exam. ☐

Make a large review chart with all the topics and fill in the details. Then use recitation to learn and review until the exam. ■

Make a practice exam, wait a few days and then take the exam. ■

If it is an essay exam, predict questions and write out the answers. ■

Get together with some friends and quiz each other. ■

Use recitation when studying so that you are practicing recalling the information as you will on the exam. ■

Get a good night's sleep the night before the exam! ■

But what if you have not been studying and learning all along? You are in trouble, but here are some ideas:

- Identify the main ideas and make a review chart, as mentioned above. Then use recitation to practice recalling the information.

- Go over all the notes using recitation.

- There is no time to reread the book, but look at the headings, learning objectives, and practice questions.

- Think about previous exams and predict questions for this exam. Then answer the questions.

- Get a good night's sleep the night before the exam!

AND—after the exam, evaluate your preparation and make any necessary changes to your study habits for future exams.

You will be taking exams throughout the remainder of your undergraduate career and on into graduate school, if you continue in your education. Here are some additional tips for preparing for a major exam:

First you need to know the following:

What information will the exam cover?

What is the format? Multiple choice? Long or short essay? Online or on paper?

Do you have all the class notes and materials that you need to study?

Are there any things that you do not understand that will be on the exam?

Next, organize the material you need to learn:

What are the major topics? How many are there? Write down these topics either in a list or in a review chart with the topics across the top of the page.

Go through your material and write down the sub-topics within each major topic.

As you are doing this, be sure to combine information from your textbook and lecture notes.

Finally, begin to learn each topic as explained in the previous entry.

Here are some specific strategies to use while learning the information:

Recitation—after reviewing the information, cover it up and restate it in your own words from memory.

Organize the material into study guides, review charts, time lines, flow charts—whatever format suits the information you need to know.

Predict exam questions and then answer them.

- Form a study group and either quiz each other or divide up the material and teach each other.

- If quizzes are available online or in the textbook, be sure to take those.

The night before the exam, get a good night's sleep. Your brain will not function properly if you are tired.

Good luck—but "good study" is better!

My students often struggle with motivation. Some students find that there are so many fun and distracting things to do that academics come last. Other students have an extremely tight schedule with family and work obligations and find it hard to squeeze in studying. One way to keep motivated and on track is to set goals for yourself. An effective goal has three characteristics:

It must be measurable.

It must be attainable.

It must have a definite time limit.

Goals can be **short-term** (day or week), **medium-length** (month or semester), or *long-term* (one or several years).

Here is a plan for setting a weekly goal:

Set your goal for the week on Sunday night or Monday morning. Make sure it fits the above three criteria. **1**

Write it down. **2**

Put it where you can see it daily. **3**

At the end of the week, evaluate how you did and set a new goal or the same goal for the next week. **4**

Sample Goals

Too vague, unattainable:
I will study harder.
I will never miss another point on an exam.
I will earn better grades.

Attainable goals:
This week I will go to all my classes.
This week I will review my notes after every class.
I will study one hour a day for my exam next Friday.

What is your goal for the week? Write it down and tape it to your bathroom mirror. Good luck!

Aristotle said, "We are what we repeatedly do. Excellence, then, is not an act but a habit." What are your habits? How are you spending most of your time? How we spend our day-to-day time determines what we will achieve in life.

Think about what you are doing on a daily basis and ask these questions:

- Are my daily activities moving me toward my goal?

- Am I doing the best job I can at whatever task I am preforming?

- Would I be proud of how I spend my time if someone shadowed me for a day?

- What activities and things do I repeatedly do? Are they positive to my future?

Are there any changes you think you should make that will help you achieve your goals and dreams? If so, pick one and start today.

Be sure to do something every day to move yourself toward your goal!

*"Success, real success, in any endeavor demands more from an individual than most people are **willing** to offer—not more than they are **capable** of offering."* —James Roche

One of the most important ingredients in academic success (in any success, really) is what you are **willing** to do to be successful. How much time and effort are you **willing** to devote to achieving what you want? What other activities are you **willing** to sacrifice or skip in order to have more time to study or work on a project?

As stated in the quote above, the difference between the successful and unsuccessful person is not his or her capabilities, but his or her **willingness** to work hard to achieve success.

As midterm exams approach, how much effort are you **willing** to devote to your learning? What outside, social activities might you have to skip in order to have enough time to prepare for your exams?

Take a minute to make two lists:

What do I need to do in my classes to prepare for mid-terms?	What non-academic activities can I skip to allow more study time?

The semester is close to half over, but the results of your efforts will stay with you forever.

48

Studying:
Active vs. **Passive**

Everyone is busy preparing for midterm exams. When you are thinking about how to study, consider how you can use active strategies versus passive strategies.

Active strategies are when you are manipulating the information either through writing, shuffling note cards, or making concept maps, review charts, time lines, etc.

Passive strategies are when you are simply reviewing or thinking about the material with limited involvement.

Obviously the active strategies are going to be the most effective way to get the information into your long term memory. Here are some examples:

Active Strategies: *(more effective)*	Passive Strategies: *(less effective)*
Outline textbook material	Reread your notes
Annotate reading material	Reread your textbook
Make study cards	Study while watching television
Create review charts, concept maps, time lines	
Rewrite notes	
Combine lecture and textbook notes in a new outline	
Take online practice tests	
Write answers to study guides provided by professor	
Form questions—write them and then the answers	
Form a study group and quiz each other	

Each institution has different procedures for midterm grades. Sometimes professors only have to tell you if you are earning a D or F, while others calculate all of the grades.

You should have a general idea of how you are doing. If you do not get a midterm grade in the course and feel you are not doing well, you should still go and **speak with the professor.**

If you do get a low midterm grade, **speak with the professor.**

Here is what you want to know:

Is there a chance for me to pass?

What do I have to do to pass? What grades do I need to earn for the remainder of the semester?

How can I improve? Explain how you have been preparing for class and ask for suggestions for improvements.

What other opportunities do I have to get points? Even though I am not a fan of extra credit, you must ask to know if there is any available!

If there is no chance of passing, then your decision is between an F and withdrawal (W) from the course. In both cases you will not receive any credits for taking the course, so if this class puts you fewer than 12 credits for the semester or 24 for the entire year you will need to explore the possibility of summer school. Generally a W is much better than a F. The credits and zero quality points will not be calculated in your grade point average (GPA), so it is much easier to get a decent GPA. An F in a course really lowers your GPA. The other issue is retaking the course. If you withdraw, you could take the course during the summer at an institution closer to your home. If you fail a course, you generally have to take it again at the same school in order to do a D/F repeat (if that is an option at your school).

NOTE: Be sure to connect with your advisor before making any decisions, and find out your school's policies.

If you find yourself in this situation, do the best you can to minimize the damage, determine what went wrong, and work in the future to avoid the problem. Of course, it goes without saying that the best practice is to be working hard and avoid D and F grades!

Even if you are doing well (but not at the A level), this is the time to reflect on how you are studying and preparing and see if you can make some changes. It is important to know how close you are to the next grade level. Is there a chance to move up? Again, evaluate how you have been preparing for class and think about strategies for improvements.

Remember: There is no "good-grade fairy" who will "bonk" you on the head with her wand and magically raise your grade. You have to do it yourself!

Welcome to the second half of the semester. Here are a few things to think about:

Are you happy with the way things went the first half?

How successful were you academically?

How could you improve academically?

What challenges are there in this second half? Major papers? Exams?

What plans can you make to meet these challenges successfully?

There is still plenty of time to improve if you are not satisfied with your work so far. Take advantage of your professors, peer educators, counselors, and others on campus. They are there for you and want you to succeed.

If things have gone well the first half, resolve to stay the course and maintain a high level of excellence.

Each semester, fall and spring, has its own special challenges. In the fall we are heading toward the holidays, so there will be a festive atmosphere on campus as well as distractions from home. In the spring it is the weather—once it is warm and sunny outside you will be tempted to skip class. Don't do it! In either case, the last half of the semester will fly by. Stay dedicated and on course. Keep your semester and long-term goals in mind.

Enjoy and stay dedicated!

When you are learning new material, it is a lot easier if you understand **The Big Picture.** You will be able to see how all the information fits together, and it will be easier to remember the small details. The Big Picture is important at all stages of learning, from the first exposure to the material through reviewing for an exam. Here are some strategies that are helpful:

Before starting to read a textbook chapter, preview it by looking at the learning objectives or chapter outline, the headings, the bold print, etc.

When you are reading anything, be thinking not only about the details, but also about the overall article.

Look for the organization of the information. Are there two opposing viewpoints in the article? Is it in chronological order? Does it compare and contrast two or more topics? You must know this before you can understand!

When taking lecture notes, think about how each individual lecture fits into the current unit or the entire semester of material.

When you are reviewing for an exam, go through your notes to see the major topics. Make a large review chart with all the topics listed. Look for common themes and fill in the sub-points.

Pause every so often and consciously think about The Big Picture and how everything relates and fits together.

The next time you read, study, or attend class, think about The Big Picture. Then fit the new information you are gaining into that organization.

It is helpful for learning if you can make connections between what you are trying to learn and what you already know. Once you are in subjects related to your major this is quite easy because each class relates to what you hope to do after graduation. But sometimes students in the liberal arts (or general education) courses don't see the reason for taking certain classes.

Actively look for connections. Did your history professor mention something that relates to what you studied in psychology? Can you relate what you are studying in class to a book you read or movie you saw? Any kind of association or connection helps. Remember that it does not have to be academic—can you connect what you are learning in class to a vacation you took or something your friend said in high school?

Likewise, when reading in your textbooks, be sure to look for connections to the class lectures and vice versa. In each class you are putting together a body of knowledge and all the pieces (lectures, textbooks, articles, videos, speakers, etc.) should fit together. You have to be open to the connections. If you are, you will find them!

There are many reasons why college students put off doing what they have to do or should do. One of the main reasons is that there are so many other fun things to do instead! It is really hard to say "no" to your friends and miss out on the immediate fun in exchange for studying that will show you little benefit until a test or quiz. But we all know that it is the **day-to-day** studying that makes the difference in the **long-term learning**.

Here are some ideas to motivate yourself to study on a regular basis:

Think of banking time ahead—if you study regularly and keep up with everything you may not have to say "no" when an unexpected event comes up.

Look ahead to what is happening on the weekend, and then back up your planning. Start with Monday and schedule time to study so that all your work is done before the event. You are using the event as your reward for getting everything done.

Sometimes you just have to say "no." It is easier if you see the long-term goal you are working toward. Write your goals on an index card and post it on the bathroom mirror so you will read it every morning. Then do things every day to move toward that goal.

Get on a regular study schedule or routine. For example, go to the library every day at the same time or when you have a break between classes.

Avoid going anywhere near your bed in the middle of the day if napping is a problem!

Remember that breaking any habit, especially procrastination, takes **dedication** and hard **work**. The first few times you work instead of putting it off will be uncomfortable, but once you are in the habit or routine it will be easier—**not easy, but easier.**

There really is not a lot to say about distractions except that you have to remove yourself from them. Learning takes extended concentration. You cannot learn if you are constantly checking your e-mail, going on Twitter, playing a game on the computer, etc. You have to pay attention to what you are doing—one thing at a time.

Sometimes this is as easy as disabling Facebook for an hour, turning off your phone, going to the library away from your friends, or turning off the television. (I know this sounds extreme—but you really can do this!) You are not isolating yourself for the rest of your life, just for a short period of time. If someone expects to be in constant contact with you via texting or Twitter, tell them you are studying for a specific length of time and then reconnect with them when you are done.

Other times the distractions are more intrinsic—inside your own mind. These types of distractions could include family or financial worries, grade concerns, contentious relationships with friends or a significant other, or other problems. These are a bit harder to deal with, but it can be done.

One idea is to physically write down what you are worried about the then set the list aside and study. This physical act helps you mentally set the worries aside and learn.

Another idea, strange as it seems, is to designate specific times when you will actively worry about the problem, and then visualize yourself moving forward from the worry.

It might also help to think of a plan of action—when and how will you deal with this.

Finally, consider going to the health center or counseling office at your school and talking with someone not connected with your concern. It is a big help just to verbalize what you are worrying about and put it in perspective.

The good news is that if you eliminate distractions and pay attention to your studies, you will be more successful and more efficient, and you will be done sooner!

Overcoming the
Mid-semester Slump

If you have been reading one entry a day, the semester is about half over. You may have had a short fall break, or you may not have had any break but there's a week off at Thanksgiving to look forward to. Many students (and professors) are tired. It is not uncommon to feel a let-down of energy and motivation about this time.

Here are some ways to rejuvenate yourself:

■ Review your motivations. Why are you here? What are your goals? Why is what you are doing important?

■ Evaluate how well you are taking care of yourself. Are you getting enough sleep? Enough exercise? Are you eating healthy food?

■ If you are feeling stressed or overwhelmed, plan something fun and relaxing over a weekend—not the whole weekend, though, just a part of it!

■ Sometimes it is easier to work solidly through a weekend and get on top of things when you know you have some "down time" the next weekend. There's no better way to relieve the stress of feeling overwhelmed than to just settle in and get the work done.

■ Above all, keep your focus on the big picture. The semester will end soon enough, and you will have some time off!

At least for me, in a day or so I usually have my energy and motivation back. Just remember to enjoy the journey!

Here are some quick time management tips using either an "old-fashioned" kitchen timer or the timer on your phone:

If you are going to study, read, or review for a short period of time, set the timer for the allotted time instead of constantly checking the clock to see how much time you have left. This way your brain is free to concentrate on the material instead of always calculating how much more time you have.

If you are having trouble studying a subject you do not like, set the timer for 20 minutes and only study for that length of time. You can stand anything for 20 minutes. And tomorrow do another 20 minutes!

If you can't maintain your focus or concentration, set the timer for five or ten minutes and work for that time period. Take a short break and then go for another five or ten minutes. After a day or two, lengthen the time by a few minutes. Keep lengthening the time until you have trained your brain to stay focused for a longer period.

Good luck! Remember that your success is in your control.

Common Mix-ups

When writing essay exams or formal papers, there are words that students commonly confuse. Spell-checkers do not help because these are still proper words, but students mix them up and use the wrong one. As an educated person, you need to know how to correctly use these words.

Quiet: not noisy
Quite: completely or to a considerable extent

Due: a date when something should be completed
Do: an action or a task

Their: possession
There: location
They're: contraction of "they are"

To: in the direction of
Too: more than enough or also
Two: the number 2

Suite: two or more rooms
Sweet: a sugary taste

Keep these in mind the next time you are writing a paper. Your professor will have an easier time following your ideas if his or her thoughts are not interrupted by incorrect words.

Plan Your Work
and Work Your Plan

This is one of my husband's favorite sayings. While it might be annoying after you have heard it a hundred times (ask our daughters while they were living at home), it contains is a lot of wisdom!

We are slightly past the halfway point of the semester. Deadlines for long-term projects are looming on the horizon, papers are coming due, midterm grades have been posted, Thanksgiving or spring break is ahead, and then comes finals week. It can seem overwhelming! At my university, students also have the pressure of registering for next semester classes.

One strategy is to take some time to look at the remainder of the semester as a whole. Get a calendar and write down what assignments are due and when, the dates of all exams, the dates for any break, and finals week. Then, plan out when you will do the work that needs to be done. If you have to work over a few weekends, that is okay! Hard work is very satisfying when you can see that the end is in sight. And it is a lot less stressful when you have a plan to get everything done.

So now here comes my husband's saying. You have done the first part; all you have left to do is the second.

Plan your work and work your plan!

More Effective Academic Reading:
Two Quick Steps

If your academic reading needs a pick-up, here are two quick strategies you can add that will make a big difference in your comprehension and retention of the material. You have read about them before, but sometimes a reminder is helpful.

1. **BEFORE** you start to read, **PREVIEW** the material.

- Look through the chapter or article and look at any headings or bold print.

- See how the information is organized—think about the big picture of the piece.

- Look at any new words defined in the margins.

- Read the learning objectives or the chapter outline.

- Look at the pictures, charts, graphs, etc. (otherwise these will distract you during the actual reading).

- If it is a trade book, read the back cover, any note from the author, table of contents, whatever information is there to help you see (again!) the overall organization of the book and the big picture.

2. **AFTER** you are done reading the text, **REVIEW** what you have read.

- Look through the chapter again and reread the headings.

- Reread any notes you have taken.

- See if you can answer the learning objectives.

- Think about what you read and see what you can restate in your own words.

These two quick strategies can make a big difference in your effectiveness as a reader. Give them a try!

It takes repeated exposure in a variety of formats for information to become firmly implanted in your long-term memory. This is why cramming for hours the night before an exam does not work. To truly learn information, you should:

- Review often

- Use a variety of study strategies

Distributed Practice means that you are spreading out your studying and reviewing over an extended period of time. This is above and beyond the regular reading and lecture note review that happens on a class by class basis. If there is something that you find difficult, or if there is a large amount of information to learn, the best thing you can do is distribute the learning over time.

For example, you might make study cards for your Spanish class and review them 20 minutes at least 5-6 days per week. If history is the class you are struggling in, you could use the same time frame and:

- Make and review study cards for that class,

- make a review chart and use recitation to remember what goes in each category,

- take one topic a day from your notes and review it using recitation, or

- outline or write the information in the learning objectives from the beginning of each chapter and then recite.

The important thing is that you are reviewing for about 20 minutes almost every day of the week during the semester. **AGAIN, Distributed Practice is above and beyond** your regular reading and reviewing!

61

How to Handle Low (*or lack of*) Interest in a Subject

If you are at a liberal studies institution, you are taking classes covering a broad number of topics. One problem students sometimes encounter is a lack of interest, which can lead to missing class and not studying. Unfortunately the end result is often a low or failing grade and then the need to take the class <u>again</u>. Here are some things you can do to combat low interest:

- Try to find something in the course to relate to your own life or major.

- Remind yourself of your overall goal and see this class as one step closer to that goal.

- Picture yourself as an educated, informed person who has a broad range of knowledge.

- Remind yourself that it is easier to pass the course the first time rather than <u>paying and taking it again</u>.

- Act as if you are interested in the course. Think about what you would do if you were interested and then act that way. (I know this sounds a bit strange, but my students have reported that it works!)

Keep in mind that you are in charge of your own learning and mind. YOU control what you do and how you study.

Section Four
Final Third of the Semester

Things to think about:

Using your senses while learning

Habits

Thanksgiving Break

Test-taking strategies

Finals week and final exams

Here are six things beginning with R that are important to learning:

Recitation: Restate some of your class material in your own words from memory. You are practicing recalling the information just as you will on an exam. Plus, if you can restate something in your own words, you truly understand it.

Repetition: Learning does not happen all at once, it takes multiple exposures.

Review Soon After: Go over the information in your lecture notes while it is still fresh and before you forget it. Use this time to be sure the information is clear and correct.

Rest: Sleep is important for effective learning, and it is a time for new knowledge to consolidate in your memory.

Re-energize: Keep motivated! Review your short-term and long-term goals frequently.

Re-organize: Check your calendar, syllabi, and schedule daily for exams, due dates, meetings, deadlines, etc. When reading and studying, be sure that you see the organization of the material you are learning.

What are your
Habits?

Take a minute to review your **habits**. What are you doing on a daily basis? Remember that you need to have **habits** that will lead you to success. Below are some positive **habits** that will lead you to success and some negative ones that will get in the way of your success:

Positive: *Heading for Success*	Negative: *Roadblocks to Success*
Going to the library to study after class	Going back to your room after class and taking a nap
Reviewing notes immediately after class	Not looking at your notes until the night before an exam
Getting a good night's sleep	Staying up late and hanging out with friends
Eating healthy food	
Exercising	Not keeping track of your assignments
Building in relaxation and "fun" time	Getting to class late
Having goals for the day, week, and semester	Skipping class
Getting to class early and reviewing the previous notes	Partying too much
Finding help when it is needed	

It is important to periodically examine what you are doing and reinforce positive activities and change negative ones. What positive habits have you incorporated into your days and weeks? What habits might you change before they are too ingrained? Be sure that how you spend your time, energy, and effort is getting you to your end goal!

One way you can increase your learning is by using your various senses (sight, hearing, touch, or movement) while studying. Here are some ways to incorporate the <u>visual</u> sense in your learning:

Create charts or graphs.

Add color to your notes, charts, study cards, etc.

Draw pictures.

Look at pictures or videos on the Internet.

Pay attention to diagrams.

Create your own diagrams.

Visualize what you are reading or studying.

If you are studying a person, find a picture so that you know what they looked like.

You even might find that you can visualize your study aids when you are taking an exam!

If you like color and visuals, these suggestions will make your learning and studying more effective and enjoyable.

65
Learning Through Your Senses:
Auditory

Think about how you like to get directions to somewhere you have never been. Do you like to follow a printed map or itinerary? Perhaps you remember best if someone verbally tells you where to go and maybe you repeat the information back to them. If this second way seems the best, you may like to learn through your sense of hearing. There are several study strategies you can use that involve sound and words:

■ Read your textbooks or notes out loud.

■ Read your textbooks or notes to some sort of rhythm.

■ Sing your notes to a rap beat.

■ Tape yourself reading your course materials and then listen while driving or exercising.

■ Form a study group and explain the class information to each other or quiz each other.

■ Teach the information to someone else.

■ Decide how you work with background noise. Background noise can be fine while studying; just don't let it overpower your thoughts. And remember that you will be taking the exam in silence.

■ Attend class, of course. It's important that you attend all classes so that you hear your professor explain the information and so you hear your classmates' discussions.

Many students like to be on the move—they don't like to sit still. They get restless during long classes and have a hard time paying attention. They don't like to sit and read or listen for a long time. If they want to learn something, they prefer to do it themselves as opposed to reading the directions or having someone tell them what to do. If this is you, here are some ways to add large and small muscle movement into your studying:

Make and use study cards. You will like the manipulation aspect.

Take notes, rewrite notes, make charts, and create graphs and study guides—you are using small muscles!

Likewise, annotate when reading. The small muscle movement of writing will help keep you engaged.

Take your review chart and study it while on the treadmill or exercise bike.

Tape your notes and listen while walking or running.

Make use of small segments of time by carrying your study cards with you.

Try to avoid three-hour, once-a-week classes if possible. If you must take a long class, be sure to get up and walk around during the break.

When studying, take breaks every 30 minutes or so. (By "break" I mean a few minutes to walk around, not two hours to hang out with friends!)

Seek out classes with a lab component or where students do projects as opposed to exams.

Any way you can add movement will help you stay on task and learn.

You may have noticed in the three previous entries that there is a lot of overlap. For example, study cards work for a student who likes visual and color as well as for the student who likes large and small muscle movement. Listening to a recording of your notes while you are walking appeals to the student who likes auditory learning as well as the student who likes muscle movement.

Do not confine yourself to just one way of learning. The more ways you can work with the information, the better you will understand and retain it in your memory. Also, you need to be able to learn in a variety of situations and under different circumstances. So be creative and have some fun. What different ways can you think of to work with the information you need to learn?

Here are some more ideas:

- Sing your lecture notes to a beat while dancing around your room (auditory and movement).

- Draw pictures to illustrate an idea or concept (visual and movement).

- Color-code your study cards; then say the answers out loud as you go through them (visual, auditory, and movement).

- Find an unused classroom and draw diagrams on the board (visual and movement).

- Take your notes and textbook to a different location, like a coffee shop or restaurant, and study there (visual and movement).

- Exercise with a classmate and quiz each other (movement and auditory).

- Go to educational online sites to hear and watch someone else explain the information (visual and auditory).

- Watch videos/documentaries about the material (visual and auditory). (Be careful about fictional accounts.)

The point is to do different things. Don't get used to only one way of studying.

Mnemonics are quick tricks you can use at the very beginning of learning. The strategy helps you remember something that is long or difficult. Mnemonics are for material you need for a short period of time or information you want to remember but don't often access in your memory.

Some of the more common ones are:

Please excuse my dear Aunt Sally or PEMDAS
This helps you remember the order of operations in a math problem (parenthesis, exponents, multiplication, division, addition, subtraction).

Roy G. Biv
The order of the colors in a rainbow (red, orange, yellow, green, blue, indigo, violet)

Homes
The names of the Great Lakes (not in order of size) (Huron, Ontario, Michigan, Erie, Superior)

Every good boy does fine
The notes on the lines in the treble clef (E, G, B, D, F). The notes in the spaces are F-A-C-E.

You can create your own mnemonics for things you need to learn. Take the first letter in each of the words, and use them to create a new sentence or word you will remember. If order is important, you cannot mix up the letters; otherwise, feel free to make any word you can.

If you are studying in your major, eventually you will not need the mnemonic. Trust me—a mathematician does not stop to think about their dear Aunt Sally when working problems. But at the beginning of learning they are quick, easy, and fun!

Final Weeks
of the Semester

As the semester draws to an end, there are several things you should start to think about:

Are any of your grades on the borderline? If so, start to put extra effort into studying for that class, over and above your regular studying.

When are your finals? If you have several in one day, there may already be a policy in place to help you move one of them. You can also speak to one of your professors to see if they are giving the same exam at a different time.

Do you have all the materials you need for the finals?

Do you have any major assignments due during these last weeks or as a final? If so, have you started to work on it? If not, start NOW!

If you are living in the dorms, when do you have to be out? When can someone come and get you if you need a ride?

The last weeks of the semester go by very quickly. Start now to stay on top of your work and studies so you can enjoy either the holidays or the spring weather while still maintaining your academics.

Toward the end of one semester, a student asked what he needed to earn on the final exam in order to earn a B in the course. The answer was that he needed almost a perfect score on the exam to reach that goal. Unfortunately, he missed the main essay question on the exam and ended up with a C. The student only missed the final grade of B by a few points, which he could have earned on other exams or projects anytime during the semester. What he did not understand is that his final grade was a reflection of <u>all</u> of the learning and work done throughout the semester, not just on the final.

Sometimes only one point makes a difference between two letter grades. Professors differ in whether they will bump a student up to the higher grade. If they are willing to do so, it would only happen if the student worked hard throughout the semester and had good attendance. In most cases professors will <u>not</u> do this because there will be other students in the same situation. So, keep in mind that even the smallest assignment is important. Always do your best and submit your best work.

Even in a course that only has a midterm and a final, you now know that your grade will reflect how hard you worked and how much you learned throughout the <u>entire</u> semester. You cannot just study the day or two before an exam and expect to be able to learn and understand everything.

Keep in mind it is the day-to-day work and learning that is important, and everything will count as your professor is calculating your grade.

Knowing
vs. **Understanding**

As we approach finals, think about the difference between knowing and understanding. If you just review and reread your lecture notes and textbook, you will "know" the material. You may be able to recognize the information on an exam if it appears in the same words as your notes or textbook. But if the information is restated in different words, appears in a different order, or if you are asked to apply the information learned in class to a new situation entirely, you will not be able to do it.

You need to learn the information past the point of knowing and to the point of understanding. You can do this using several strategies:

- Use recitation—can you restate the information in your own words?

- Teach someone else—can you explain what you have learned to someone?

- Manipulate the information in various study guide formats.

- Relate the information to what you already know.

- Apply the information to a new and different situation.

Gaining understanding is especially important in courses like psychology and business. The exams in these courses usually give you new scenarios and ask you to apply the information that you learned to the different situations.

Adapt your study strategies so that you understand the material.

This is a good time to review the importance of class attendance and effort. Here is a portion of an e-mail I sent to some absent students to remind them about the importance of class attendance and effort in their studies:

1. **Learning is cumulative**—you can't just pop in and out of a class. One class builds on another. When you are absent, you miss the continuity of the subject and cannot easily follow the material. Also, if you miss too much, you do not feel a part of the class the next time you are there.

2. **Success is habitual**—you must do good work constantly, not just occasionally. You cannot expect to earn good grades on quizzes and exams if you are not doing good work all along.

★★The people who are successful in life are able to maintain their efforts over time. The semester is only 14 or 15 weeks long—stay strong to the end!

Student Scenario

One of my students asked me if he should withdraw from his psychology course. He said that he earned a 52% on the first exam and a 54% on the second and was afraid of failing the course. He reported that he had studied for the first exam by reviewing his notes several times, and he studied even "harder" for the second exam.

What do you think actually happened?

The problem was that he just did more of the same thing when preparing for the second exam. When he said he "studied harder," he actually meant that he just reviewed his notes a few more times, but he did not really do anything different when preparing for the second exam.

What should he have done?

He should have used a variety of strategies to learn the material. Learning requires varied and repeated exposure over time. For example, he could have:

- Made study cards for the vocabulary
- Made a study guide to help him understand the information
- Joined a study group and discussed the information
- Used recitation—restating the information in his own words to be sure he knows it beyond the same words used in his notes
- Made sure he understands the examples used in the textbook

The happy results:

This student used several more study strategies for the third exam and earned 75%. He stayed in the course and earned a passing grade.

The most successful readers use a variety of strategies to help themselves understand and remember what they are reading. This is particularly true of academic reading. Here is a review of some strategies that you will find helpful and fairly easy to add to your reading:

Preview: *Before you start to read, look over the assignment to get the big picture.*

What is it about?

How is it organized?

Are there any interesting visuals?

Look at the bold print words—do you understand them? Are they defined somewhere?

Read the learning objectives at the beginning of the chapter for guidance about what you are to learn.

Monitor your comprehension: As you read, be aware of your attention and understanding. If either one lags, reread or take a step back and see where the information you are reading fits into the overall topic of the assignment.

Visualize: Can you picture what you are reading? This will depend on the topic, of course. But, can you see a picture of what the author is describing?

Recite: Stop after each paragraph or section and restate what you just read in your own words. Can you do that? If yes, continue on. If no, go back and reread and try again.

Annotation: Writing notes in the margins expands recitation.

Review: This small step will make a huge difference. After you are done reading, take a few more minutes to think about what you have read.

Happy Reading!

Study = Learning + Review

I was talking with a student about what it means to "study." He had "looked over" his science notes, but was that really studying? My reply was that what he did was "review" and he had yet to fully "study."

So, what is the difference?

There are two parts to studying:

1. **Learning**—this is your initial work with the information and is quite in depth. You can use a variety of strategies to learn the material. These include:

- Reading and note-taking
- Rereading
- Making study guides such as concept maps, charts, study cards, or questions and answers
- Recitation—restating in your own words from memory
- Rewriting
- Working through practice problems

2. **Reviewing**—this is what you do to keep the information fresh in your memory after you have learned it. Strategies to do this include:

- Recitation using the study guide you made during the learning stage
- Distributed practice—reviewing the information for short periods over time
- Rereading notes and/or study guides
- Practice problems
- Taking any practice quizzes or tests available through the textbook or your professor

You can see that this is quite time consuming, but learning does not happen quickly. It takes time and effort. Keep up the hard work!

The semester is drawing to a close. You probably have a few weeks of classes followed by a week of final exams left in the semester. Everyone is feeling the time crunch. Many long-term assignments are coming due and finals are looming in the future. Everyone feels a bit overwhelmed at this point.

One way to deal with this is to make a calendar for the remainder of the semester. You can do this on the computer or by hand, but it works best if you can see the entire schedule on one page. Add the following:

Due dates for assignments (think about setting a false, early deadline)

Dates and times of finals

End-of-semester, holiday celebrations or outdoor activities you want to enjoy

Study sessions, tutoring times, or supplemental instruction sessions

Anything else that is happening that is important to you

Just a hint: If it is fall, the time between Thanksgiving and the end of the semester is very hectic—fun, but hectic! If it is spring and the weather is changing from winter to warm spring weather, you will want to be outside. Plan ahead and organize your work so that you can enjoy the last weeks of the semester!

77

Everyone thinks they can do two things at the same time: listen to a lecture and text, check text messages or e-mail and review lecture notes, read a textbook and watch television. The truth is that your attention is just bouncing back and forth between two (or more!) things. You are much more efficient if you do just one thing at a time, and then do the next thing.

Here is an experiment that I do with my classes:

1. Write the following two lines, but the first time write them alternating letters and numbers (M, 1, u, 2, l, 3, t, 4 . . .). Time yourself to see how long it takes.

Multi-tasking is worse than a lie.
1, 2, 3, 4, 5, 6, 7, 8, 9, 10, 11, 12, 13, 14, 15, 16 on through 28

2. Now write the complete sentence and then the complete list of numbers and time yourself again. You will see how much quicker you wrote both the second time.

This is just a small illustration of how trying to do two things at once leads to not doing either one well. This carries over to your studies and distractions. You need to give your full attention to your work; save the other things until you are done.

Many of us have one entire week off for Thanksgiving break. This is a wonderful time to relax and visit with family and friends. BUT—it can be harmful for learning. If you have any work to complete over break, if you have an exam shortly after returning from break, or if you have a difficult class, taking one week off from studying can be disastrous! Forgetting happens very rapidly, so it is important to spend some time studying over break. Here are some suggestions:

Plan before you go home when you will study and do your work. Don't just think that you will do it when you "have the time." Set specific times now.

Write down your plans and tell someone. This will help keep you accountable.

Consider going to your local library or coffee shop. Go somewhere away from the distractions of your home, the TV, and your bed.

If you have some friends at home from your school, make plans to meet and study and then go out for lunch.

Do your studying early in the break. You are more likely to do it then than at the end.

Review every day. To prepare for an exam shortly after you return to school, make a study guide or study cards and review for 20 minutes or so every day. You will be amazed what a difference that makes. This is also a good idea if you have a class that is very demanding or if you are struggling (either to pass or earn an A).

Particularly if your break is an entire week and you do not review over break, you will have to start learning from the beginning when you return to classes.

Keep in mind that there are just a few weeks of classes after break, and then you go into finals! Be sure you are caught up with your work and studying so that you have plenty of time to prepare for final exams.

Be thankful that you have the opportunity to further your education. **Happy Thanksgiving!**

After Thanksgiving Break

As you return from Thanksgiving break and look forward to the end of the semester, there are several things to consider:

- Is all of your work complete? Have you missed any quizzes, exams, or projects? Check your syllabus to be sure.

- What is due between now and final exams?

- When are your final exams? If you have several on one day, can you make any changes? Is there a system in place at your school to address this?

- What will the exams cover? Are they cumulative or on the final unit of the semester?

- What social events are happening? Which are important, and which should you skip in favor of studying?

The semester went by quickly, and these final days will move even quicker. Be sure to look at the big picture and manage your time so that you can enjoy yourself as well as be successful.

Thinking about the purpose of exams from both the professor's and the student's point of view can change your attitude about tests and the way you react to them. Here are some ideas:

The professor schedules exams in order to:

Evaluate the individual students and assign grades.

Give the students motivation to pause, review, and study. (We know that learning requires periodic review in order to become consolidated in your memory, and we also know most students are unlikely to do this without the motivation of an exam!)

Evaluate the learning of the entire class to determine if he or she needs to reteach a topic.

Evaluate his or her teaching strategies. Perhaps they will approach a topic differently the next semester.

From the student's point of view, after an exam he or she can:

Evaluate his or her understanding of the material.

Evaluate his or her study and learning strategies.

Evaluate his or her test-taking strategies

Evaluate his or her career decision if the course is in his or her major and he or she struggled with the material.

So you can see that exams serve many purposes for both the professor and the student. By thinking about exams in this way, you can change your attitude about the entire testing process.

Good luck as your finals are approaching!

There is no substitute for knowing the correct answer, but you still have to communicate that answer to your professor so that he or she knows that you know. Here are some tips:

- Read the ENTIRE question.

- Pause and think about the answer.

- Mark up the question. Number the parts or underline important words.

- Consider making a brief outline before starting to write.

- If it is a multiple-part question, answer each part in order.

- Use signal words to help the professor follow along. If there are three parts, use words like "first, second, third." If the professor asks for examples to prove your point, start the sentence with "for example."

- Restate the question in your first sentence to keep your answer direct and on topic.

- If you have time, reread your answer. Be sure that it makes sense. Put yourself in the place of the professor and see if it is clear.

- Keep in mind that you are the writer and your job is to be clear for the reader. Don't assume the reader/professor will "know what you mean" because he or she obviously knows the material. Your job is to clearly explain the information and to demonstrate how well you know the material.

As stated previously, there is no substitute for studying and knowing the correct answer. But having some test-taking strategies definitely can help. Here are some tips for multiple choice questions:

Read the prompt carefully. Be sure you know what it is asking. ■

Don't plan on simply "recognizing" the right answer when you get to it. Here's why: ■

The information will be worded differently than your lecture notes and the textbook. It also probably will be in a different order than in your lecture notes. ☐

There are almost no "give away" answer options. All the possible answers are from somewhere in the unit—they just do not all pertain to the question you are answering. ☐

Read ALL of the options before making a choice. There may be several possibilities, but you want the BEST one. ■

Use the process of elimination. ■

Be careful and slow down if the prompt has the words NOT or EXCEPT. This changes the question. In some cases, you are now looking for the WRONG answer. ■

Don't trust "C." The old adage of "when in doubt chose C" does not work. The professors have heard it also. ■

Remember: sometimes it is true that the longest answer is the correct one. ■

Be sure the answer grammatically fits with the prompt. ■

Don't be afraid to skip questions. If you do not know an answer, you can skip it and keep the question in your mind. It is very possible that a wrong answer later on will trigger your memory for the correct answer to the one you skipped. (Just be careful to be on the correct number on the bubble sheet. Getting off by one number is disastrous!) ■

Good luck! But remember—hard work beats luck.

When should you start to study for final exams?

This is a trick question with two correct answers:

1 Right now!

2 After each class as you learn your lecture notes.

When you prepare for a major exam, review all of the information you previously learned and take a step back to see the big picture.

Here are some ideas:

- Start several days or a week before the exam.

- Look at the major topics to be covered in the exam and write them on separate pieces of paper or in the heading area of a large review chart.

- Go through your notes and the book and add the major points under each topic.

- Include some examples for each topic, especially if this is a class where you will be expected to apply the information to new situations.

- Be sure you know the format of the exam. Then predict exam questions.

- Notice how the topics all fit together. Are there connections the professor might ask you to make?

- Take one topic per day and thoroughly review or relearn it.

- Review all the topics every day leading up to the exam. Remember to use recitation—cover your notes and restate the information in your own words from memory.

Do NOT stay up all night to study! You will not remember anything, and your memory won't work well for days.

This is an undesirable and avoidable situation, but here you are, so what should you do?

You will not be able to review every small detail. First, go through the material and identify the major topics. Then, do the following:

Write each topic at the top of a page or on a large (5"x7") index card.

1

Working with one topic at a time, go through each topic and outline the next level of topics, leaving some spaces in between.

2

Go back again and write important information under each subtopic.

3

Do this for each of the major topics.

4

Now focus on one card at a time and begin to learn the information.

5

Depending on how much time you actually have before the final you can go deeper and deeper into the material. If there's time, go back and reread your notes after reviewing your basic outline on each major topic. Depending on how much of the final is from the textbook, go back and skim the book, again according to each major topic you identified.

You should NOT

Stay up all night

Take no-doze or some other drug

Panic

Next semester remember to review and learn your notes after each class. Then when it comes time for the final exam it will be a breeze.

Twas the Week before Finals
and All through the Dorms...

For most of you, finals are next week, and the pressure is mounting. Papers and projects are due. Exams are scheduled. Professors are squeezing in the last important information they want you to know. AND you possibly have to pack all or some of your belongings to be ready to go home.

There are a few things you can do to handle everything:

- Be sure to get enough sleep.
- Eat healthy food and get some exercise.
- Schedule some social time to say goodbye to friends, but not too much.
- Look at your final schedule and start your study plan NOW!

For each of your classes that have a final, check the following:

- When is it and where? If it is in a different location than the classroom, make sure you know where it is and how to get there. (NOTE: At most schools your schedule is different during finals— classes are not meeting and the exams may be at a different time than the class.)
- What will it cover? Is it cumulative or just on the final unit of the course?
- Do you have all the information you need? Are your lecture notes complete?

Start your study plan now. Break the information into smaller topics, and review one each day until you have covered everything. Every other day or so, go back and quickly review the information you studied so far. If needed, look at previous entries in this book for some other learning strategies you can use.

A final note: Students are very tempted by "book buyback." Be absolutely sure that you are done with the book before you sell it. If they are buying a limited supply and you are afraid to wait, consider copying the pages you need first. If the book will be used next semester, you might consider selling the book yourself for more than the book buyback price but less than the used book price at the bookstore.

Good luck! (But, if you are well prepared, you won't need luck.)

You have made it through the semester and all you have left is finals week. Every year is different—some years you may have a lot of papers due, others you may have major exams in all of your courses. Whatever is happening at your school and with your finals, here are some survival tips:

DON'T

Stay up all night. This is the worst thing you can do! It will take you the rest of the week to recover, and you will not be able to think clearly.

Hang around with people who will make you stressed and anxious.

Give in to pressure to party—you will see these friends again!

DO

Make sure you know the time and location for each exam. Double check! Then plan to arrive early.

Eat healthy and exercise.

Make a study plan so you have enough time to prepare for each exam.

Maintain a positive attitude.

Ask for help if you need it. Many schools have a policy regarding how many exams you can have scheduled in one day. Your professors probably are also willing to help you out if all your exams are scheduled in only one or two days.

Take some time—but not too much—to relax during the week.

Look forward to some break time when finals are over!

If you have kept up with your studying and worked hard, you will do well. You will see the results of your work soon!

Good luck! And enjoy a job well done!

Section Five

After the Semester has Ended

Things to think about:

What went well this semester

What would you like to change

How to handle a grade dispute

Your finals are over and you are headed home for the semester break or summer. Here are some things to consider:

Keep all your papers and returned exams until you receive your final grade for each course. If you think there was an error, you will need these to prove your point.

Keep all your syllabi. If you ever decide to transfer, the new school may want to see them in order to determine if the credits will transfer.

If you were unable to sell your textbooks, consider selling them yourself at the beginning of the next semester. You may be able to sell them at a price below the used book price at the bookstore but higher than you would have received during book buyback.

Over the break consider reading a book that relates to your field. Go to your local library for suggestions.

Many schools offer short summer or winter sessions online. If you take a class somewhere else, be sure it will transfer before registering. Your own institution can help with this.

Reflect on what went well this semester. Think about how you will continue to do the same thing next semester.

Reflect on what you could have done better. What changes can you make next semester, and how can you implement these changes?

Use this time to recharge your motivation. Reflect on your goals. Visualize yourself in the career you are considering.

Relax! Rest! Enjoy time with family and friends!

Grades are Posted:
Now What??

Now that you have your semester grades, what's next?

If you are happy with your grades:

- What did you do well this semester?

- What did you do to be successful in your classes and when studying?

- How can you transfer those same work and study habits to the next semester?

- Is there anything you didn't do but should have? (This would be a great time to write a reminder to yourself and pack it with your belongings for next semester!)

- What courses are you taking next semester? Which ones will be more challenging? What can you do to be successful in those classes?

- Enjoy some well-deserved relaxation time!

If you are NOT happy with your grades:

- What went wrong? (Don't entirely blame others—what was your responsibility?)

- What could you have done differently? (Again, consider making a list and putting it where you will find it next semester.)

- What can you do to fix things? (Maybe change your next semester schedule and add a D/F repeat?)

- Review your goals. Why do you want to go to college? What sacrifices are you willing to make to be successful in your future classes?

- Take some time to renew your goals and your determination to be successful!

This is the perfect time to reflect and review. Then resolve to do well or even better next semester!

If you think you received a grade that is incorrect, there are several things you can do. Keep in mind that most professors want their grades to be correct and will be more than willing to talk about your grade and fix any error made on their part.

If you do not understand why you received the grade you did, you should contact your professor. (Some may not reply to e-mails, so for those you will have to wait until the beginning of the next semester.) Be polite, write that you expected to receive a higher grade and state why. If after he or she replies you still think there was an error, your institution has some policies in place to work this out. **1**

Be sure to keep all the graded exams and work that was returned to you in case there is a dispute. **2**

Be sure to keep a copy of all correspondence you have with the professor, even if they do not reply. **3**

It is well within your right to go to the professor's office at the beginning of the next semester and ask to see your final exam. **4**

The key is to be polite. Most professors are very willing to correct any mistake they may have made. **5**

If, after speaking with your professor you still think the grade your received is incorrect, look at the catalogue or student handbook for your school. There are policies and procedures in place for you to pursue. **6**

Section Six

Looking Forward

Things to think about:

Roadblocks and strategies for overcoming them

How to raise your grade point average

Spring fever and spring break

Online and condensed classes

One of the nice things about education is that you get to wrap up a semester, reflect on what went well and what you could improve, and then you get a brand new start.

Here are some common problems that students encounter and some ideas for positive changes:

Roadblocks to Success	Strategies for Change
Waiting too late to begin to study	Review and learn notes after every class and all notes at least once a week
Not going to class	This is simple—resolve not to miss any classes. Make a weekly chart with all your classes listed and then cross them off as you attend. See how many perfect weeks you can have. (If you must miss, contact the professor and be sure to attend the next class.)
Too much social life and not enough academic life	At the very beginning of the semester, make a weekly plan. Schedule your study times during the day and early evening. Get into the habit of studying immediately after class. Go to the library instead of to your room or apartment.
Unorganized	Have a separate notebook for each class. Keep all the papers for each class together. Stop and think before leaving your room to be sure you have everything you need.

Missing assignments and exams	Get a daily planner and monthly calendar and write everything down. Go through each syllabus at the beginning of the semester and write all exams and major assignments on the monthly calendar as well as the daily planner. Write short-term assignments in your daily planner as they are assigned. Be sure to get into the habit of looking at the planner and calendar daily.
Lack of interest and motivation, Part I	Set goals for the semester; write them down and post them where you will see them daily. There are several types of goals: Daily: a to-do list Weekly: for example, "Go to all classes." Semester: for example, set a grade point average you would like to achieve
Lack of interest and motivation, Part II	If you have a clear career goal, imagine yourself working in that field. Think about how what you are learning in class might pertain to that career. Even a course not directly in your major field will prepare you to be a successful, well-rounded person in that field.

Lack of interest and motivation, Part III	If you do not have a clear career path, make one of your goals this semester to explore your options by going to the career services center at your university. Read course descriptions in your college's catalog and see which ones sound interesting to you. In the meantime, imagine yourself at graduation filled with a feeling of accomplishment. No one is motivated all the time, but successful people have some strategies to help keep going. Dreaming of graduation day is one that will keep you focused
Choosing short-term pleasures over long-term goals	This is hard. No one wants to miss out on immediate fun and instead study for something that will not happen for a month or more. But that is what it takes. If you begin to study daily and plan ahead, you should not have to miss too much. But sometimes you just must make the choice to stay home and study. In the end the rewards will be greater, so keep your mind focused on the long-term goal.

NOW it's your turn. Think about your previous semesters. What changes can you make to find academic success or to enhance the success you are already having? If your academic success is at the level you want, then enjoy it and continue!

One aspect of college that is interesting is that each semester is different. You have to set new habits and routines each semester. So, as you approach the beginning of the new semester, here are some things to do and consider:

Make a weekly chart of your classes and any other weekly responsibilities or commitments you have. Then decide:

- What is the best time for studying? How will you fit in the number of hours needed?

- When will you sleep and exercise?

- When will you eat? If you have back-to-back classes, does the food service offer bag lunches?

- It is easiest if you get into a good routine from the beginning of the semester.

Look at your various classes. Are there any that will be particularly challenging? How will you handle them? Is there tutoring available on your campus? Where and when?

When you receive the syllabus for each class, put the major papers, assignments, and exams on your monthly calendar so you know in advance how to organize your time.

Make sure that you start the semester at the top of your game. Remember that the first week always seems easy, but things get hectic and stressful quickly. Start off running!

There is *not* one quick fix for raising one's grade point average. It involves day-to-day effort in multiple areas.

The quickest way is to retake classes in which you earned a low grade and replace that low grade with a higher grade the second time around. At my institution this is called D/F repeats and can only be done for classes in which you earned those grades. Be sure to follow the procedures at your institution—each is different and has different rules. Is goes without saying that you must do things differently the second time—more time spent studying, more varied strategies, etc.

Then resolve to earn higher grades in <u>all</u> of your classes the next semester. Here is a review of how to achieve that goal:

Use a daily planner and write down all assignments.

Use a semester calendar to keep track of large assignments and exams. LOOK AHEAD so that you are preparing in advance.

Review your lecture notes as soon as possible after EVERY class.

Do something else with the lecture notes to learn them—recitation, study guides, self-made pre-test, etc.

Read whatever is assigned. If it is a long assignment, annotate and/or take notes. If it is a short assignment, read it twice.

Start to study for exams at least one week in advance. (Keep in mind that this is in addition to reviewing and learning your notes after every class.)

Take advantage of tutoring or supplemental instruction offered on your campus.

Talk with your professor if you do not understand something from the class.

As you see, the answer is not ONE thing, but MANY things. Raising your grade point average is a slow process. You will have to work to keep your motivation and to remind yourself that each small thing you do on a daily basis will be important in the end. Keep focused, keep working, and don't let up!

Take a Break
over Spring Break!

Spring break presents unique challenges for college students. It can be a time to be carefree and relax or to work as many hours as possible to earn more cash for the rest of the semester. BUT, many of you will have papers to write or exams to study for. It is guaranteed that you will not feel like studying over break, but it must be done. How can you fit that into your schedule and still do what you want to do?

Here are some ideas:

- First, get as much done as possible before you go home. And when you go, be sure to take everything you need!

- Second, before you go home, plan what days and times you will study. Write them down. Then stick to the plan.

- Tell some other people at home your plan. They can help you stay on task.

- Remember that the longer you go without reviewing the material from your classes, the more you will forget. Then when you return you will have to study even more to relearn the material. Review information from classes about 20 minutes per class several times over break. This will minimize forgetting.

- It will also be helpful if you can study in a location that is more academic—perhaps your local library or coffee shop.

- If you've never studied at home before, pick one location (dining room table or a desk in your room) where you will always study.

- If you are going on a vacation or service-learning trip, make some review charts and study cards to take with you, and find some time to review them often during the trip.

- If you have an exam the day or so after returning to school, you will have to do more intense study distributed over the week. This is where studying throughout the semester will pay off! Spring break is a time to relax and rejuvenate to prepare for the remainder of the semester.

With some careful planning you can do that and also keep up with your studies.

Relax and enjoy!

Don't Succumb to Spring Fever!

Depending on where you are, the weather in the spring semester can change surprisingly from cold to warm. It is amazing how quickly students transition from heavy coats, scarves, and hats to shorts and flip-flops. However, with just a few weeks left in the semester, there is no time for spring fever. Here is what you can do to still enjoy the nice weather without falling behind:

Keep up with your time management. Write down everything you must do and plan when you will do it.

Work ahead (especially on a rainy day) so that when there is a particularly nice day you have some extra time to enjoy it.

If you can find an isolated spot, study outside. Just be sure you are away from distractions.

Take your exercise outside—run, walk, or play a game.

Keep your eye on the prize! The important thing is to finish the semester strong, not to be outside with your friends.

Enjoy yourself and continue to work hard!

What are your plans for the summer? If you are planning on working, you still need to keep up your learning skills. There are several almost painless things you can do:

Play Free Rice at www.freerice.com or other learning games on the internet. You can enhance your vocabulary, practice math problems, brush up on grammar, review your Spanish or French, and more. If you are taking a second language, a good amount of forgetting will happen if you do not review over the summer. This website is an easy way to do that. The same goes for math— if you are in a math progression to reach the final course for your major, this website will keep your math skills current and help you avoid backsliding over the summer.

Read. Read the newspaper, a current popular novel, whatever interests you. Again, this will help keep your critical reading and thinking skills at a high level.

Pay attention to information you run across that pertains to your major. If you are looking for them, you will find print and online articles as well as news reports that will help you stay current in your field. This is a lifelong habit you will be following when you are working in your career.

Be aware of opportunities for service and leadership. These will not only provide great experiences, but also look good on your résumé.

Speaking of résumés, keep in mind that you may be asking your current employer for a reference in a few years. Also, even if your summer job is not in your field, what can you learn about dealing with people in a professional setting?

Finally, relax and enjoy some well-deserved time off!

One way students can lighten their semester load, catch up after a major change, or graduate early is by taking summer classes at an institution close to their home and transferring the credits to their college or university. Here are some things to consider:

If you think you might want to do this, talk to your advisor so that you can plan ahead and "save" some classes to take at another school. There may be a transfer office and a list of approved classes students can take elsewhere and transfer in.

Usually students who want to do this take the liberal studies or general education requirements elsewhere and take their major classes at their home school. Check to see if there are any regulations about this.

Be sure you have approval to take the course BEFORE you register and pay.

In most cases just the credits will transfer, not the grade, so this is not a good way to raise your grade point average. Usually only a "C" and higher will transfer.

If you failed a class, you probably have to retake it at your home school.

This is a good way to stay on track if your major has a high math or other requirement and you have to take some lower level courses to catch up your skills.

Keep in mind that these classes will more than likely be just as rigorous as the course at your own college, but you might have an easier time if you are only taking one course at a time.

Sometimes there is a rule that you must complete a certain number of your final credits at your home institution. Check on this.

A Word about Technology and Research

One thing that technology has changed is the way we do research. You can access your library's website and other sources from anywhere at any time of the day or night and retrieve full documents on your computer screen or other device. This is much easier than the old card catalogues your parents or grandparents used and the endless stacks of journals they had to search through to find the issue they wanted.

Here are a few things to remember when it comes to technology:

There is a technology office on your campus where you can go for help.

The role of librarians has also changed, and they are now experts at using search engines and doing online research.

Now that you can get instant information from around the world, confirming sources is even more important. You will have to do more research and be current with the respected publications in your field to be sure the information you have found is accurate.

Anyone can publish anything they want. Check, check, check!

Allow time for glitches—things will break down or not be accessible, and if you have waited until the last minute you will be in trouble!

Save your work in the cloud so that you can access it anywhere and you don't have to worry about crashed computers or flash drives.

Many students take classes online. There are many different formats; some have recorded lectures, some are all reading, some require some face-to-face time. You, as the learner, have to be flexible and adapt your learning strategies to the situation. There are a few specific tips for online success:

Don't think the course will be easier because it is online. Instead of regular access to a professor in a classroom setting, much of the learning will be on your own.

Time management is crucial to your success in this situation. The tendency is to put off the work. Treat the course just like a regularly scheduled course. Have specific times when you will do the work. Get into this habit or routine and stick with it until the course is over.

Be sure to monitor your understanding and learning. Don't ignore difficulties or unclear information. Contact the professor and ask questions. Other students in the class are also a resource.

There will probably be discussion groups and the professor will be monitoring who contributes, so contribute early and often.

Don't assume that because the quizzes and exams will be online you will have time to look up the answers. They will be timed and possibly monitored through the camera on your computer, so you have to study and prepare just as you would for a regular classroom exam. A comprehensive review chart would be very helpful but don't plan to rely on it.

Be sure to utilize all of your learning and study strategies. Again— remember that you are responsible for your own learning and for your completion of the assignments. Many students thrive in online classes. The work can be flexible and fit into varied schedules. As long as you have sufficient motivation, time management, and learning skills, you will do well!

Many classes offered outside of the regular semester format are in a time period shorter than the normal semester-length class. There are advantages and disadvantages to this format:

Pros:

- You can focus on only one or two classes. You are not spreading out your study time over four or five different subject areas.

- The class usually meets every day, so repetition is built-in.

- Even while working very hard, you know it is for a brief time—you can see the end.

Cons:

- You must stay on top of your studying; you cannot take even one day off.

- There exams and/or assignments scheduled almost weekly.

- You are learning and studying a semester's worth of information in a short period of time, so there is a lot to learn. You will be very busy.

Here are some tips for success:

- Mentally prepare for the work. Plan on studying every day, including weekends.

- Remember to use a variety of study strategies.

- After each class, learn the information from that day and review all the previous information.

- Don't miss any classes.

- Be sure to keep track of assignment and exam dates.

- Dedicate yourself to the course for the duration—make it your primary focus.

- Schedule a fun activity for when the class is over, so you have something to look forward to.

Many people find quotations a fun way to keep themselves motivated. Consider finding a quote you like, writing it on a notecard, and posting it where you will see it every day. The first one by Aristotle is on the bulletin board above my desk both at work and at home. The rest are a few of my students' favorites:

We are what we repeatedly do. Excellence then, is not an act, but a habit.
   —Aristotle

Before anything else, preparation is the key to success. —Alexander Graham
   Bell

Success demands singleness of purpose. —Vince Lombardi

I know the price of success: dedication, hard work, and a devotion to things you
   want to see happen. —Frank Lloyd Wright

Success seems to be connected with action. Successful people keep moving.
   They make mistakes, but they don't quit. —Conrad Hilton

Success is a result of consistent practice of winning skills and actions. There
   is nothing miraculous about the process. There is no luck involved.
   —Bill Russell

Success doesn't come to you…you go to it. —Marva Collins

Success, real success, in any endeavor demands more from an individual than
   most people are willing to offer—not more than they are capable of offering.
   —James Roche

When I thought I couldn't go on, I forced myself to keep going. My success is
   based on persistence, not luck. —Estee Lauder

Always bear in mind that your own resolution to succeed is more important
   than any other one thing. —Abraham Lincoln

It's supposed to be hard. If it wasn't hard, everyone would do it. The hard…is
   what makes it great. —Jimmy Dugan from A League of Their Own

Many people fail in life, not for lack of ability or brains or even courage but simply because they have never organized their energies around a goal.
    —Elbert Hubbard

Time management quotes

Nothing is so fatiguing as the eternal hanging on of an uncompleted task.
    —William James

Procrastination is opportunity's assassin. —Victor Kiam

Someday is not a day of the week. – Janet Dailey

A year from now you may wish you had started today. —Karen Lamb

Do not squander time for that is the stuff life is made of.
    —Benjamin Franklin

Conclusion

Congratulations to those of you who have successfully completed your first semester! Take some time to think about what you have just accomplished and enjoy your success. Use that success and what you have learned for motivation as you continue your academic path.

If you are further along in your academic career and are not having the success you had hoped for, keep going and stay strong! Take some time to evaluate your work so far, congratulate yourself on your triumphs and resolve to change anything that is holding you back.

No matter what method you used to read this book – whether by reading daily entries while taking classes, the entire book before starting college, or skipping around to different entries that interested you – I hope you found it useful and inspiring. Remember that learning is a process and that what you do daily will, in large part, determine the outcome. Also, remember to enjoy the daily journey and work hard so that you have no regrets.

About the Author

 Arden B. Hamer is an educator, reader and author, recently retired from Indiana University of Pennsylvania where she taught Critical Reading/ Critical Thinking and Learning Strategies. She earned her undergraduate degree at Grove City College and her master's and doctoral degrees at the University of Pittsburgh. Reading and learning are her passions. You can follow her blogs: www.ReadtoEnrich.blogspot.com and www. StudytoSucceed.blogspot.com.

Acknowledgements

Working with Tom Costello and Word Association Publishers continues to be a wonderful experience. Special thanks go to April Urso (cover and interior design) for her expertise and understanding of my goals and Donna Wenzel for insightful editing suggestions. My former colleagues at Indiana University of Pennsylvania are great and have provided inspiration and ideas. Darlene Pabis, my co-author on a vocabulary textbook series, lit the writing spark! Sally Lipsky and Susan Dawkins gave me invaluable advice. Most of all, my husband and family provided encouragement and motivation.

WA